P.S. I LOVE YOU TWO! A SEQUEL

Lynda Milligan & Nancy Smith

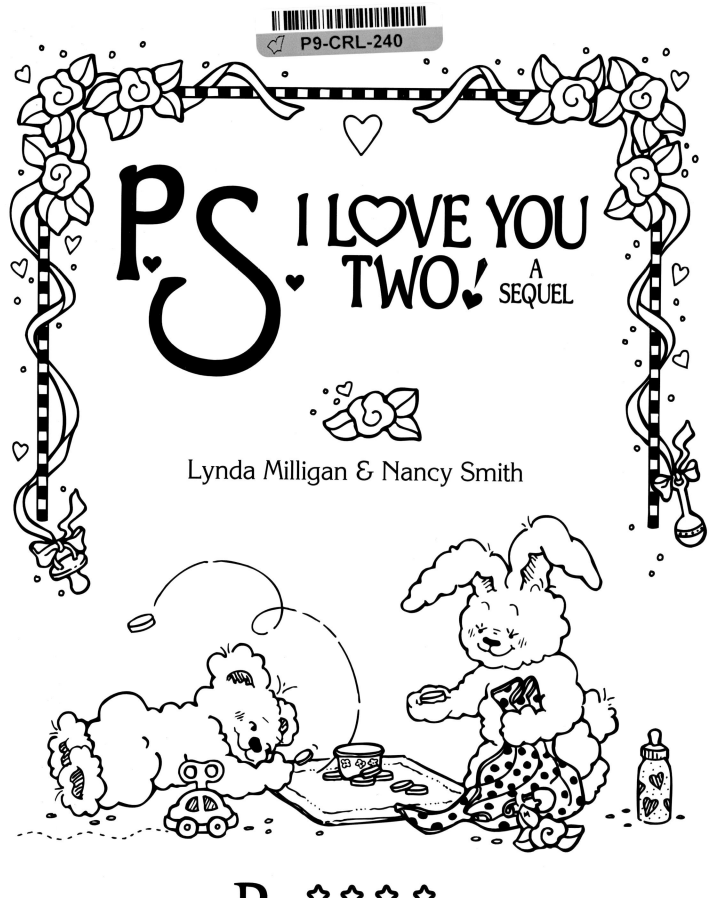

POSSIBILITIES®

…Publishers of *DreamSpinners*® patterns,
I'll Teach Myself® sewing products, and *Possibilities*® books…

Credits

Editing—Sharon Holmes
Illustration & Cover Design—Marilyn Robinson
Photo Styling—Susan O'Brien
Technical Drawing—Sharon Holmes, Susan O'Brien
Consulting—Jane Dumler
Photography—Brian Birlauf

Special Thanks

To Chris Scott for her patient proofreading.
To Joanne Malone and Debbie Andrew for their sewing and quilting skills.
To our fine staff at Great American Quilt Factory, Inc. for their help and suggestions.
To Blue Rabbit Ltd. gift shop for supplying us with accessories for photography.
(Traditional folk art accessories are available from Blue Rabbit Ltd. by calling 303-843-9419.)
To Colorado North Company LLC–South Platte Company LLC–Builders of Sanford Homes
for allowing us to photograph in their model homes.

...Publishers of *DreamSpinners®* patterns,
I'll Teach Myself® sewing products, and *Possibilities®* books...

P.S. I Love You Two

Library of Congress Catalog Card Number: 96-70473
ISBN: 1-880972-26-3

Table of Contents

Introduction

Dear Friends,

As we said in the original *P.S. I Love You*, nothing is more wonderful than welcoming a new baby into the world with his or her very own quilt—a one-of-a-kind security blanket. *P.S. I Love You Two* inspires you even more to make distinctive and treasured heirlooms.

P.S. I Love You Two is a comprehensive book that shows you what fun it is to create a special environment filled with warmth, love, and caring. The quilts appeal to quilt makers of all skill levels. Fabrics range from sweet, muted pastels to homespuns to contemporary, bold brights. Quilts are shown in room settings that spark imagination for your special nursery.

Complete directions, full-sized templates, and fabric charts for seventeen quilts, most sized from little or wall hanging to twin, are included. A full range of accessories is given—bumper pads, crib sheet, dust ruffle, pillows, birth record, rocking chair cover, and coordinating valance. The *Quilting Techniques* section includes basic information on all phases of hand and machine quilt making.

Personalized, individual gifts create a bond of love that nurtures both the maker and the recipient. *P.S. I Love You Two* continues the quilting tradition begun in *P.S. I Love You* by saying, "You are my special one!"

Happy Quilting!

Nancy & Lynda

P.S. Several of the quilts are made with *Simple Gifts*, fabric we designed for Peter Pan Fabrics, a division of Henry Glass, Inc. These quilts are shown on pages 33, 39, 43, and 45. We had great fun designing and working with this fabric, and we hope it will be available for a long time. We also know that these quilts will be just as beautiful in fabric selections you choose.

Quilting Techniques

Fabric Preparation

Fabrics made of 100% cotton are highly recommended for quilting. All washable fabrics should be laundered before being used in a quilt. Determine if fabrics are colorfast by hand washing separately in detergent and warm water. If the water remains clear, fabrics may be washed together. If any fabric bleeds, wash it separately. If fabric continues to bleed, discard and select another fabric. After checking for colorfastness, wash fabrics in a washing machine with warm water and a mild detergent; rinse well. Tumble dry, as most shrinkage occurs in the dryer. Press, using steam and spray sizing if necessary.

Hand Applique

1. Make plastic templates from patterns without including seam allowances.
2. Place template on right side of fabric, avoiding selvage, and draw around it.
3. Cut pieces out, cutting ³⁄₁₆″ to ¼″ outside drawn line.
4. Baste under all edges not overlapped by another piece by folding edges under on penciled line and basting in place with a single thread.
   a. Clip seam allowance on inside curves and points, allowing fabric to spread.
   b. Clip inside angles up to seamline. When appliqueing these angles, take small overcast stitches to prevent fraying.
   c. Miter outside points less than 90° in three separate folds. Fold down point; fold one edge to seamline; fold other edge to seamline. It may be necessary to trim corner before folding to reduce bulk.
5. Pin or baste pieces to background fabric using pattern as a guide.

6. Using thread to match, applique. Work stitches from right to left. Hide knot under applique or on back. Bring needle out through folded edge of applique. Insert needle into the background directly under where thread emerges from fold and bring it up approximately ⅛″ away, catching only one or two threads of the folded edge of the applique. Repeat.
7. To end, bring needle to back and knot off.

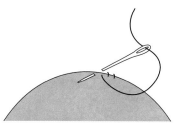

Machine Applique

FUSING WEB METHOD

1. Trace patterns the reverse of the direction wanted onto smooth, paper side of fusing web. **Note:** Patterns in this book have already been reversed.
2. Avoiding selvage, press fusing web to wrong side of fabric with rough side facing fabric. Cut out shapes.
3. Peel off paper. Position applique on background fabric, and fuse in place with an iron. If design is layered, arrange all appliques before fusing.
4. Satin Stitch: Place tear-away stabilizer under background fabric. Use a very short stitch length and a medium zigzag stitch width. Loosen top tension as needed to keep bobbin thread from being visible on top of work. Keep threads of satin stitch at right angles to edge of applique by pivoting as needed. To make tapered points, reduce stitch width while sewing. To tie off threads, bring stitch width to zero

and take 6-8 stitches next to satin stitching. Tear away stabilizer.

5. Invisible Open Zigzag: This is a fast way to secure edges of fused appliques without creating an outline of thread as in satin stitch. Use a narrow stitch width and a medium-short stitch length to create a small, open zigzag. Use nylon monofilament thread as the top thread only.

Hand Piecing

1. Make templates from patterns without including seam allowances. Hint: Mark proper grain line on each template.
2. Draw carefully around templates on wrong side of fabric. Allow ½″ between templates and at least ¼″ from each edge of fabric. Avoid selvage. Mark corners clearly and accurately. Make sure to flip template over for reversed patches (example: asymmetrical triangle in Pinwheels quilt).
3. Cut pieces from fabric, cutting approximately ¼″ outside marked line. Marked line is stitching line.
4. Place pieces right sides together, matching and pinning at corners and intervals along marked lines. All pins should be placed at right angles to the marked sewing line. Remove the corner pin and insert the needle at this point. Take a stitch, then a small backstitch, then sew with a short, even running stitch, checking from time to time that the marked lines on both front and back match. Remove pins as it becomes necessary. Sew to the end of marked line and backstitch. Do not sew seam allowances down; instead slide needle under seam allowances from point to point. This allows seam allowances to be pressed to either side. Assemble into units.

Pressing

In patchwork, seam allowances are pressed to one side or the other. The standard ¼″ seam allowance used in patchwork makes it difficult, if not impossible, to press seams open. In addition, the quilt is actually more durable if seams are not pressed open. It is usually preferable to press seams toward the darker fabric. If this is not possible, make sure dark fabric seams do not show through the quilt top by trimming a scant amount from the dark seam allowance. Press patchwork block on the back first, using steam and a gentle, up-and-down motion. Swinging the iron back and forth tends to distort and stretch patchwork. Then turn block over and press gently on the right side. When pressing border seams, press all seams toward outside edges.

Machine Piecing

CUTTING WITH SCISSORS

1. Make templates with template plastic—include ¼″ seam allowances.
2. Draw around template on wrong side of fabric, avoiding selvage. Cut out on the line using very sharp scissors. Watch for units that require reverse pieces (example: asymmetrical triangle in Pinwheels quilt). Hint: Fine sandpaper is a nice surface to use for marking.

CUTTING WITH THE ROTARY CUTTER

1. Square Up
   a. Begin by laying wrinkle-free, double-folded fabric on a cutting mat. Position it so the single fold and selvages are at the bottom and one raw crossgrain (selvage to selvage) edge is at the right.
   b. Using a transparent rotary cutting ruler marked with a right angle, match up the top edge of the ruler (or one of the right-angle lines) with the fold of the fabric.
   c. Hold blade flat against right edge of ruler and place it just off edge of fabric closest to you. Push rotary cutter away from you to cut off right edge of fabric. The result is a straight edge from which to begin cutting strips.

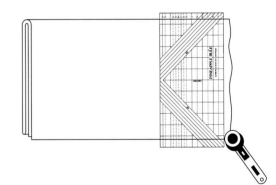

   d. Swing mat and fabric around 180˚.
2. Cut Strips
   a. Position ruler so marking for desired strip width is even with just-cut edges of fabric. Keep top and bottom edges of fabric parallel to horizontal lines of ruler.

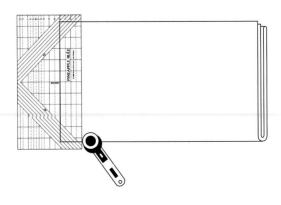

b. Cut away from you, then move strip carefully away from folded fabric to assist in placement of ruler for next cut.

c. Cut selvages off ends of strips by placing ruler on strip the same way as in Step 1—for a perpendicular cut.

Note: Strips cut this way, selvage to selvage, are referred to as crossgrain cuts.

3. Squares can be cut from strips with the rotary cutter. Be sure to include seam allowances all around patches—for 2″ finished patches, cut the squares 2½″. Layer fabric up to eight layers.

4. Half-square triangles with straight grain on the *short* sides can be cut from strips with the rotary cutter. Squares are cut first, then they are cut in *half* diagonally. To figure the size of the square, add ⅞″ to the *finished* length of the *short* side(s) of the triangle. For example, if the finished length of the short side(s) is 2″, the square is cut 2⅞″. This figuring is done for you for triangles listed in the cutting charts.

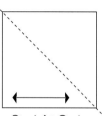

Straight Grain

5. Quarter-square triangles with straight grain on the *long* side can be cut from strips also. These triangles are used when straight grain is needed on the long side of a triangle because that side appears at the edge of a block or a strip. For this type of triangle, a square is cut in *quarters* diagonally. To figure the size of the square, add 1¼″ to the finished length of the *long* side of the triangle. For example, if the finished length of the long side is 3″, the square is cut 4¼″. This figuring is done for you for triangles listed in the cutting charts.

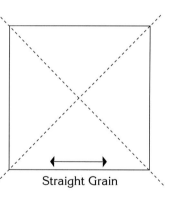

Straight Grain

6. Odd-sized and asymmetrical patches can be cut quickly with the rotary cutter by cutting around paper templates. Make sure templates include ¼″ seam allowance. Layer the fabric by 1) folding—reverse image patches will automatically be cut, or 2) stacking fabric pieces with right sides up—all pieces will be exactly the same with no reverse-image patches. Tape the pattern to the top layer of fabric with a loop of transparent tape. Using a small rotary cutting ruler (1x12″ or 6x12″), rotary cut around the paper pattern, moving the ruler as needed.

SEWING

1. Establish a ¼″ seam guide on the sewing machine.

2. Use a light neutral thread when sewing most fabrics, but if all fabrics are dark, use dark thread.

3. Using an accurate ¼″ seam allowance, place the pieces to be joined right sides together. Pin, matching seamlines, and sew with a straight stitch, 10-12 stitches per inch. Press seam allowances to one side, toward the darker fabric, unless otherwise noted.

4. To save time and thread, chain piece by sewing a seam and then immediately feeding in a new set of pieces without lifting presser foot or clipping threads. Sew as many sets as possible in this manner, then clip them apart.

5. Where two seams meet, position one seam allowance in one direction and one seam allowance in the opposing direction. Push the seams together tightly; they will hold each other in place. It is usually not necessary to pin.

6. When crossing triangular intersection seams, aim for the point where the seamlines intersect. This will avoid cutting off the points in the patchwork design.

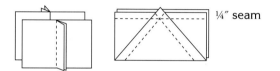

¼″ seam

7. If one edge appears to be larger, put that side next to the feed-dog of the machine so the extra will be eased into the seam without leaving tucks.

Assembling the Quilt

QUILTS SET BLOCK TO BLOCK

1. Lay out all the blocks and take a few minutes to stand back and view the arrangement. Scrap quilt blocks often need some rearranging.

2. Sew blocks together in rows using a ¼″ seam allowance. Press all seams between blocks of odd rows (1, 3, 5, etc.) to the right and all seams between blocks of even rows (2, 4, 6, etc.) to the left. When row seams are sewn, cross-seams will fit together and hold each other in place for machine sewing.

3. Sew Row 1 to Row 2, Row 3 to Row 4, Row 5 to Row 6 and so on. Then sew Row Unit 1-2 to Row Unit 3-4 and so on. By sewing row *units* together, there will be less bulk than when sewing individual rows together in order. The final row seam will connect the top half of the quilt to the bottom half.

4. Press seams between rows the same direction.

QUILTS SET WITH SASHING

Sashing strips are used to separate quilt blocks, sometimes to separate the blocks visually and sometimes to make a quilt larger without making more blocks.

Sashing With Corner Setting Squares

1. Alter the length of the sashing strips given in the directions if your blocks are smaller or larger than the size given. For example, if the blocks should have finished at 6″ not including seam allowance, but yours finish at 5¾″ not including seam allowance, cut the sashing strips 6¼″ long instead of the 6½″ called for in the directions. Sew horizontal rows of blocks and sashing strips, beginning and ending each row with a sashing strip. Press seams toward sashing.
2. Sew horizontal rows of sashing strips and setting squares, beginning and ending each row with a setting square. Press seams toward sashing strips.
3. Sew rows of blocks to rows of sashing, opposing seam allowances at either side of setting squares. Press seams toward sashing.

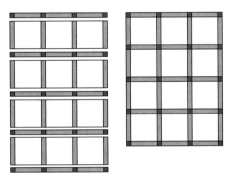

Sashing With No Corner Setting Squares

1. Alter length of vertical sashing strips to match blocks. See Step 1 of *Sashing With Corner Setting Squares*, above. Sew horizontal rows of blocks and sashing strips. Press rows well, pressing seams toward sashing.
2. Measure across the center of one horizontal row of blocks and sashing strips. Use this measurement to prepare horizontal rows of sashing. Make one less sashing strip than the number of rows of blocks. Stitch rows of blocks to rows of sashing. Press well.
3. Measure down one vertical row of blocks. Use this measurement to prepare the two vertical sashing strips for the sides of the quilt. Stitch to quilt. Press well.
4. Measure across center of one horizontal row of blocks. Use this measurement to prepare the top and bottom sashing strips. Stitch to quilt. Press well.

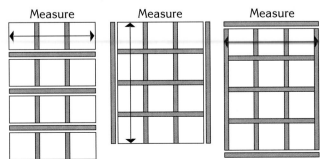

Borders

STAIRSTEP BORDERS

1. Measure and Prepare Borders
   a. To determine the length of the side borders for any assembled quilt top, measure the length of the quilt from *cut edge to cut edge* in several places. Do not measure along the *edge* of the quilt as it is often stretched and therefore longer than a measurement taken across the center. Take an average of the measurements.
   b. Stitch crossgrain (selvage-to-selvage) cuts of fabric end to end to equal the average length of the quilt top, or cut seamless borders from fabric on the lengthwise grain.
2. Pin and Stitch Borders to Quilt
   a. Fold one side border and one side of the quilt top into quarters and mark with pins. Matching marked points, pin border to quilt, right sides together. This distributes any ease along the entire edge of the quilt.
   b. Stitch border to quilt. If one edge (quilt top or border) is slightly longer, put the longer edge against the feed-dog, and the excess will be eased into the seam. Make sure all seams at corners are sewn facing the outside edges of the quilt so they can be pressed that direction when quilt top is finished.
   c. Repeat for other side of quilt.
3. Repeat measuring and stitching process for top and bottom borders of quilt.

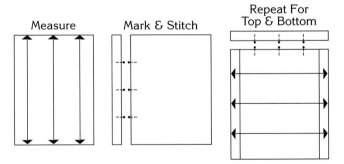

4. To measure for a second border, simply measure down the center of the first border. Stitch the side borders to the quilt, then measure for top and bottom borders.
5. Press border seams toward outside edge of quilt.

Note: Many quilters like to put top and bottom borders on first, then side borders. This simply requires reversing the order of measuring/stitching.

MITERED BORDERS

1. Measure and Prepare Borders
   a. To determine the length to prepare the side borders, measure the quilt length without borders as described in Step 1 of *Stairstep Borders* above. Add to this measurement *double* the width of *all* planned borders of the quilt, then add 2-4″ extra (yardage charts include this extra fabric).

b. To determine the length to prepare the top and bottom borders, measure the quilt top width without borders and add *double* the width of *all* planned borders of the quilt plus 2-4″ extra.

c. Stitch crossgrain cuts of fabric together, if necessary, to make the needed lengths, or cut seamless border strips on the lengthwise grain. If the quilt has more than one border, sew individual borders for each side together first to make complete border units. Press seam allowances toward outside edge of quilt.

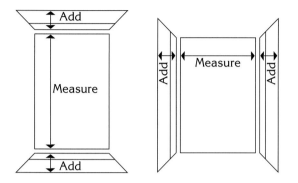

2. Pin and Stitch Borders to Quilt

a. Measure the length of the quilt without borders from *seamline to seamline* by measuring down the middle of the quilt in several places. Do not measure along the *edge* of the quilt as it is often stretched and therefore longer than a measurement taken across the center. Take an average of the measurements.

b. Find the center of the long inside edge of one side border unit and mark it with a pin. Measure from the pin in each direction, one-half the quilt length measurement, and mark with pins. These marks correspond to the corner seam intersections on the quilt.

c. Find center of quilt side by folding and mark it with a pin. Pin side border unit to quilt side, right sides together, matching corner seam intersections on quilt to corresponding marked points on border; match centers. Pin at intervals.

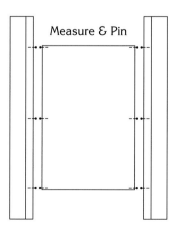

d. Stitch, beginning and ending stitching at corner seam intersections.

e. Repeat for other side, then for top and bottom.

3. Lay a corner of the quilt, right side up, on ironing board. The quilt may be pinned to the ironing board to keep it from falling off or being distorted. With borders overlapping, fold one border under to a 45° angle. Match the seams or stripes and work with it until it matches perfectly. The outer edges should be very square and without any extra fullness. Seams and pattern lines should create a 90° angle. Press this fold.

4. Flip outside edge of border with pressed fold over to other outside edge of border, right sides together; pin along pressed fold, placing pins parallel to the fold line. Open and check for accuracy before stitching. Stitch from inner corner to outside of quilt, backstitching at both ends of seam. It may be helpful to baste this seam first.

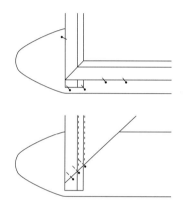

5. Lay mitered corner of quilt on ironing board right side up to see if stripes and seams match. Press. Trim mitered seam to ¼″. Repeat for other three corners.

Marking

Plan a density of quilting that corresponds to the requirements of the chosen batting. Choose to mark the quilt either before or after basting. Mark quilt top lightly with a #2 or #3 pencil. Dark fabrics or busy prints often require a white or silver pencil. Quarter-inch tape works well for marking straight lines.

Layering

For quilts that require pieced backings, piece the backing either horizontally or vertically (charts have a V or an H by the yardage of each quilt for your convenience). Allow at least 2″ to extend around entire outside of quilt top. Layer the quilt backing, right side down, then the batting, then the quilt top, right side up. Trim batting to same size as backing.

Basting joins the three layers (quilt top, batting, and backing) together in preparation for quilting. Thread basting is best for *hand quilting* projects. Use a long running stitch, catching the three layers every few inches. Start in the center and baste toward the edges in a sunburst design, or baste in a grid. Roll the backing and batting at the outer edges over to the front and baste in place with large stitches. This will protect the edges of the batting during quilting. As quilting stitches are added, basting stitches should be removed.

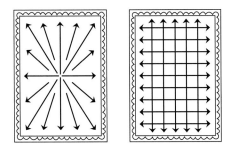

One-inch safety pins work best for basting *machine quilting* projects. Place them four to six inches apart in spots where they will not be in the way of planned quilting lines as they are difficult to remove while quilting. A rolled edge is too bulky to fit under the machine, so leave the edges flat.

Hand Quilting

Hand quilting is a tiny running stitch which creates a decorative pattern and holds the layers of a quilt together.

1. Use a single strand of quilting thread with a tiny knot at one end. A thimble is needed on the middle finger of the sewing hand.
2. From the top, insert the quilting needle through the quilt top and batting but not the backing; bring the needle up where the quilting line will begin. Gently pull thread so that knot "pops" through the top layer and lodges in the batting.
3. Plant the needle point straight down and lodge the eye end of the needle in one of the thimble indentations, releasing the thumb and index finger. Placing the thumb on the quilt surface ahead of the needle point, and exerting a steady pressure on the needle with the thimble finger, stitch, rocking the needle down and up to take several stitches at one time. Make sure the needle is penetrating all layers by placing a finger of the other hand under the quilt where the needle penetrates.

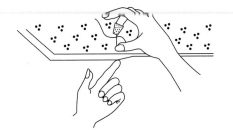

4. To end, make a knot that rests on the quilt top close to the last stitch; insert the needle a stitch length away and run it between the layers for a needle's length. Bring the needle back through the top and tug on the thread to pop the knot into the batting. Cut thread.
5. Outline quilting is quilting done ¼" from seamlines. It avoids seams and shows up well. "Eyeball" the ¼", use a pencil line, or quilt next to a piece of ¼" masking tape. Remove tape when not quilting. Quilting "in the ditch" involves stitching on or very close to the seamline and is nearly invisible from the top of the quilt. Quilt on the side that does not have the seam allowance. It holds the layers together but does not add another design element to the quilt.

Machine Quilting

1. For straight-line quilting, use an even-feed or walking foot on the machine.
2. Choose from the many threads available for machine quilting. Avoid inexpensive threads. Nylon monofilament thread can be used as the top thread for an invisible stitching line. Do not use it in the bobbin. When not using nylon thread for the top, it works best to use the same color thread in the bobbin and on the top.
3. Choose a needle with an eye large enough to accommodate the chosen thread. Some needle manufacturers offer a special quilting needle for the machine.
4. Set the machine for a stitch length of 8-10 stitches per inch.
5. Plan a density of quilting that corresponds to the requirements of the chosen batting. Plan long lines of quilting so there are fewer breaks.
6. Options for easy straight-line machine quilting:
   a. Quilt in the ditch (the lower side of a seam with the seam allowance pressed to one side) between blocks and/or sashings.
   b. Quilt straight, parallel lines either diagonally or vertically and horizontally by following some of the seams in the patchwork.
   c. Temporarily lay ¼" masking tape down on the quilt top in desired places and stitch next to it.
   d. Mark top lightly with a pencil and quilt on the lines.
7. Roll the right side of the quilt to fit through the opening of the sewing machine. Provide support for the quilt to the left and behind the machine. If quilting vertical and horizontal parallel lines, for example, stitch the vertical lines on the right half of the quilt first, starting at the edge near the center of the top border; then flip the quilt around 180° and stitch the verticals on other half. Repeat for horizontals. (See diagram in next column.)

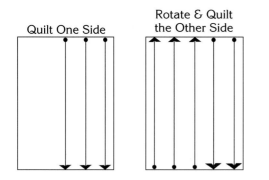

Quilt One Side

Rotate & Quilt the Other Side

8. When sewing, hold the work flat with one hand on each side of the machine foot, simulating a hoop. Keep the quilt high enough in your lap to prevent any pulling as it feeds into the machine. When stopping, leave the needle in the fabric so the quilting line will be smooth when starting up again. Backstitch at beginning and end of each line of quilting.

Tying a Quilt

1. Baste the layers with thread or pins.
2. Choose from pearl cotton, six strands of embroidery floss, ⅛″ ribbon, fingering yarn, or fine crochet cotton. Use a darning needle.
3. Tie quilt at intervals required by the batting chosen, working from the center out. Poke the needle through all layers and come up approximately ⅛″ away. Take an identical stitch directly on top of the first one. Move to the next spot without cutting the thread.
4. Repeat Step 3 until thread runs out. Rethread and continue until whole quilt is caught with these stitches.
5. Clip threads between stitches.
6. Tie a square knot at each point. Trim thread ends, leaving at least ½″.

Binding

A double binding is recommended because of its durability. Bias binding is not needed unless binding a curve.

STAIRSTEP CORNER

1. Trim batting and backing even with quilt top.
2. Cut 2½″ strips on the crossgrain of the fabric (from selvage to selvage). Stitch end to end to fit each side of quilt. Press the binding in half lengthwise, wrong sides together.
3. Attach binding strips in the same order the borders were added. Pin binding to one edge of right side of quilt, raw edges even. Stitch, using a ⅜″ allowance, and if possible, use an even-feed foot to prevent binding from "scooting" ahead. Repeat on opposite side of quilt.
4. Bring binding over the raw edge so that the fold of the binding meets the stitched line on the back. Pin binding in place on back at four corners.

5. Pin and then stitch binding to remaining sides of quilt as above, except allow the binding to extend ½″ at both ends. Turn the extended portion of the binding in before turning the binding to the back. Hand stitch binding to back of quilt, just covering stitched line.

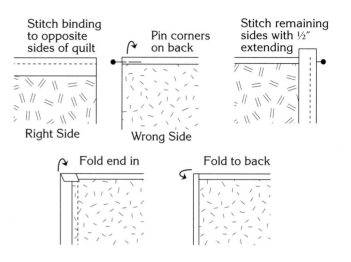

Stitch binding to opposite sides of quilt

Right Side

Pin corners on back

Wrong Side

Stitch remaining sides with ½″ extending

Fold end in

Fold to back

MITERED CORNER

1. Trim batting and backing even with quilt top.
2. Cut 2½″ strips on the crossgrain of the fabric (from selvage to selvage). Stitch end to end to fit all the way around the quilt.
3. Fold binding in half lengthwise. Leaving a 6″ tail of binding and using a ⅜″ seam allowance, begin stitching binding to right side of quilt at least 12″ from one of the corners. Stop stitching at seam intersection of first corner. Leave needle in fabric and pivot quilt 90°. Backstitch to edge.
4. Pull quilt slightly away from sewing machine, leaving threads attached. Make a 45° fold in the binding.
5. Fold again, placing second fold even with top edge of quilt and raw edges of binding even with right raw edge of quilt.
6. Resume stitching at top edge.
7. After making all four mitered corners, stop stitching 6″ from where you started. Take quilt out of machine. Lay ends of binding along unstitched edge of quilt. Trim ends so they overlap by ½″.
8. Unfold binding and pull ends away from quilt. Place ends of binding right sides together; stitch with ¼″ seam; finger press seam open. Refold binding and place it along unstitched edge of quilt. Stitch remaining section of binding to quilt.
9. Turn binding to back and hand stitch folded edge to just cover stitched line. To distribute bulk, fold each corner miter in the opposite direction from which it was folded and stitched on the front. (See diagrams in next column.)

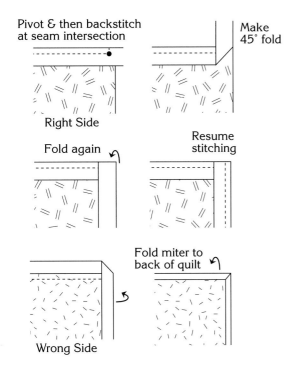

Pivot & then backstitch at seam intersection

Make 45° fold

Right Side

Fold again

Resume stitching

Fold miter to back of quilt

Wrong Side

ONE-INCH BINDING

1. Cut binding strips 5″ wide and stitch together end to end to fit each side of quilt plus 3″ extra. Press the binding in half lengthwise, wrong sides together.

2. Trim batting and backing to ¾″ bigger than quilt top (so there will be batting inside the wide binding).

3. Bind sides first. Beginning at edge of backing/batting, pin raw edges of binding even with raw edge of quilt *top*. Trim binding even with backing/batting at each end. Stitch with ⅜″ seam allowance. Fold binding over raw edge so that fold meets stitched line on backing. Press, pin, and stitch to backing by hand.

4. Repeat for top and bottom of quilt. Allow binding to extend ¾″ at both ends. Turn extended portion of binding in, then finish stitching binding to back of quilt as in Step 3.

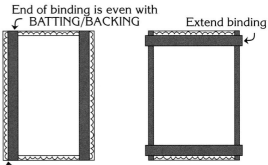

End of binding is even with
BATTING/BACKING

Extend binding

Raw edges of binding are
even with raw edge of QUILT TOP

The Quilts

Nothing says, "I love you", like a quilt. The charts for most quilts include yardage requirements for LITTLE size (wall hanging, doll), CRIB size, and TWIN size quilts. Read charts and directions thoroughly before proceeding. Directions include a scale drawing of the CRIB size quilt and diagrams for piecing the blocks. Refer to *Quilting Techniques* for help with specific quilt making methods.

Because of fabric shrinkage, cutting techniques and individual cutting discrepancies, the yardage for these quilts has been adjusted slightly upward. It is always a good idea to cut the entire quilt as soon as possible so that more fabric can be purchased if necessary. Extra fabric is included for quilts with mitered borders. Border and binding fabric have generally been listed separately from fabric specified for patchwork. This allows for individual choices. Measurements for sashing, borders, and binding are given in crossgrain (selvage-to-selvage) strips. Border width and styles may vary for different sizes of the same quilt (i.e., pieced borders on small quilts may be eliminated due to size or scale restrictions). Use the border directions in *Quilting Techniques* for measuring and stitching on borders that fit *your* quilt. Check quilt diagrams to see which border to stitch on first. Backings for crib and twin sizes have H or V following the yardage to indicate whether to piece them horizontally or vertically.

🎀 Finishing Steps for All Quilts 🎀

See *Quilting Techniques* for more detailed descriptions.

1. Press quilt top well.
2. Mark quilt for quilting if desired.
3. Piece backing if necessary.
4. Layer backing, batting, and quilt top. Baste.
5. Quilt by hand or machine, or tie.
6. Bind quilt.

Simon Says, Easy Pieces

SQUARE SIZE: 4″

Use 42-44″ wide fabric. Photo is of the CRIB size quilt.
When strips appear in the cutting list, cut crossgrain strips (selvage to selvage).
Pattern for making a template, if you wish to use one, is on page 62.

	Little	Crib	Twin
Approx. Finished Size	24x32″	40x56″	64x104″
Squares Set	6x8	10x14	16x26
Total # of Squares	48	140	416

YARDAGE

	Little	Crib	Twin
6 shirtings-style prints	⅙ yd. ea.	½ yd. ea.	1¼ yds. ea.
binding	⅜ yd.	½ yd.	¾ yd.
backing	⅞ yd.	2¾ yds. H	6¼ yds. V
batting	28x36″	44x60″	68x108″

CUTTING

	Pattern or Cut Size	Little	Crib	Twin
all fabrics	A–4½″ square	48 (8 ea)	140 (24 ea)	416 (70 ea)
binding	2½″ strip	4	5	9

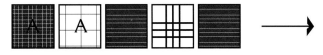

DIRECTIONS

Use ¼″ seam allowance throughout.

1. Stitch squares into rows following diagram.
2. Stitch rows together.
3. Refer to *Finishing Steps for All Quilts*, page 13. Quilts in photo are machine quilted in the ditch between squares and then again in parallel lines through the centers of the squares.

Jacks

BLOCK SIZE: 6″

Use 42-44″ wide fabric.

Photo is of the LITTLE size quilt. Diagram is of CRIB size.

When strips appear in the cutting list, cut crossgrain strips (selvage to selvage).

Patterns for making templates, if you wish to use them, are on page 62.

The square pattern is for both the background *and* the folded triangle.

	Little	Crib	Twin
Approx. Finished Size	31x38″	46x53″	68x98″
Blocks Set	3x4	5x6	8x12
Total # of Blocks	12	30	96

YARDAGE

	Little	Crib	Twin
background	⅝ yd.	1⅛ yds.	3⅝ yds.
folded triangles/blocks–scraps to total	⅝ yd.	1⅛ yd.	3⅝ yds.
folded triangles/border–scraps to total	⅝ yd.	¾ yd.	1⅛ yds.
sashing	½ yd.	⅞ yd.	2¼ yds.
border 1	⅓ yd.	½ yd.	⅝ yd.
border 2	⅜ yd.	½ yd.	¾ yd.
binding	⅜ yd.	½ yd.	¾ yd.
backing	1⅛ yds.	3 yds. H	6 yds. V
batting	35x43″	50x58″	73x103″

CUTTING

	Pattern or Cut Size	Little	Crib	Twin
background	A–3½″ square	48	120	384
folded triangles/blocks	A–3½″ square*	48	120	384
folded triangles/border	A–3½″ square	40	62	104
sashing	B–2x6½″	8	24	84
	2″ strip	5	9	24
border 1	2″ strip	4	5	8
border 2	2½″ strip	4	5	9
binding	2½″ strip	4	5	9

*Cut in sets of four of the same fabric if you want each pinwheel to have four blades of the same fabric.

To Make Folded Triangles

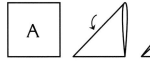

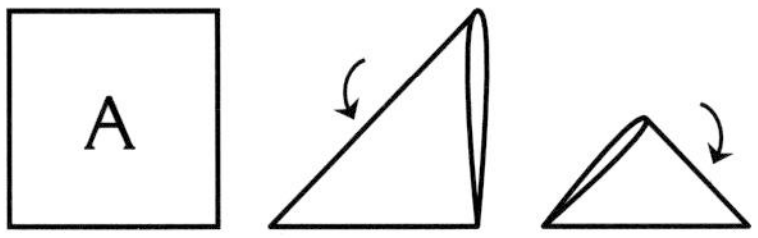

To Make One Block

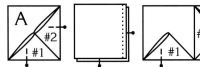

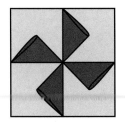

DIRECTIONS

Use ¼″ seam allowance throughout.

1. Make Folded Triangles: Fold 3½″ squares cut for block and border pinwheels in half diagonally, wrong sides together. Press well. Fold again into smaller triangles (see diagram). Press accurately and well. All of the raw edges should be lined up evenly. The triangles will have one side with a double-folded edge and one side with two single-folded edges (see diagram).

2. For One Block: With right sides together, place one triangle on a background square with raw edges of triangle aligned with one side of square (see diagram). Pin well. Place a second triangle next to the first triangle, matching double-folded edges. Make sure double-folded edges fit tightly together. Pin well. Place a second background square over the pinned triangle section, right sides together. Stitch along edge (see diagram). Open up squares and press second triangle toward second square. Make another half-block. Place two

Continued on page 48.

Color Forms

BLOCK SIZE: 6x8″

Use 42-44″ wide fabric. Photo of dark quilt is on page 80. Photos are of CRIB size. When strips appear in the cutting list, cut crossgrain strips (selvage to selvage). Patterns are on pages 65-66.

	Little	Crib	Twin
Approx. Finished Size	22x28″	45x57″	66x100″
Blocks Set	3x3	6x6	9x11
Total # of Blocks	9	36	99

YARDAGE

	Little	Crib	Twin
background–scraps at least 7x9″ to total	¾ yd.	2 yds.	5⅛ yds.
hearts–scraps at least 6x8″ to total	¼ yd.	1 yd.	2⅛ yds.
stars–scraps at least 6x8″ to total	¼ yd.	⅝ yd.	1¼ yds.
moons–scraps at least 6x8″ to total	⅙ yd.	⅙ yd.	⅓ yd.
letters–I LOVE YOU!	⅛ yd.	¼ yd.	½ yd.
border–if lengthwise stripe	1 yd.	1⅞ yds.	3 yds.
border–if not a stripe	⅜ yd.	1 yd.	1⅞ yds.
binding	⅜ yd.	½ yd.	¾ yd.
backing	⅞ yd.	3 yds. H	6 yds. V
batting	26x32″	49x61″	70x104″

CUTTING	Pattern or Cut Size	Little	Crib	Twin
background	A–6½x8½″	9	36	99
hearts	pg. 65	5	23	60
stars	pg. 65	3	10	30
moons	pg. 66	1	3	9
letters	pg. 66			
border if stripe	2½x26″	2		
	2½x32″	2		
	5x49″		2	
	5x61″		2	
	6½x70″			2
	6½x104″			2
border if not stripe	2½″ strip	4		
	5″ strip		6	
	6½″ strip			9
binding	2½″ strip	4	6	9

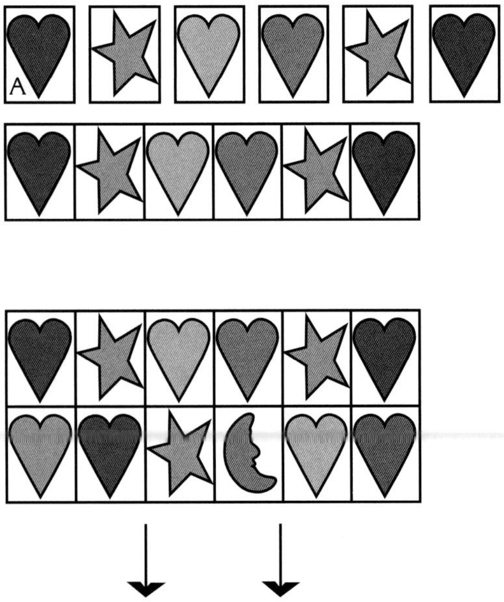

DIRECTIONS

Use ¼″ seam allowance throughout.

1. Applique hearts, stars, and moons to background rectangles. Add interest by reversing and tilting some of them.
2. Arrange blocks as desired. Stitch blocks into rows.
3. Stitch rows together. Press.
4. Stitch border to quilt. See *Mitered Borders*, page 8.
5. Applique letters to borders if desired.
6. Refer to *Finishing Steps for All Quilts*, page 13. Light quilt in photo is machine quilted in the ditch between blocks and ¼″ from appliques. Dark quilt is quilted by hand ¼″ inside each rectangle and around appliques in a variegated pearl cotton thread.

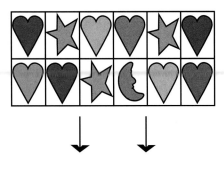

Star Light, Star Bright

UNIT SIZE: 6″

Use 42-44″ wide fabric. Photo is of the CRIB size quilt.
When strips appear in the cutting list, cut crossgrain strips (selvage to selvage).
Patterns for making templates, if you wish to use them, are on page 64.
Quilting pattern is on page 63.

		Little	Crib	Twin
Approx. Finished Size		30x42″	42x54″	66x102″
Units Set		5x7	7x9	11x17
Total # of Units		35	63	187
YARDAGE				
background		1⅛ yds.	1¾ yds.	4 yds.
stars		¾ yd.	1½ yds.	4⅝ yds.
binding		⅜ yd.	½ yd.	¾ yd.
backing		1⅜ yds.	2⅞ yds. H	6⅛ yds. V
batting		34x46″	46x58″	70x106″

CUTTING	Pattern or Cut Size	Little	Crib	Twin
background	A-6½″ square	12	20	54
	B-4¾″ square	17	31	93
	C-3⅞″ square*	10	14	26
stars	A-6½″ square	6	12	40
	C-3⅞″ square*	24	48	160
binding	2½″ strip	4	5	9

*Cut these squares in half diagonally to make triangles.

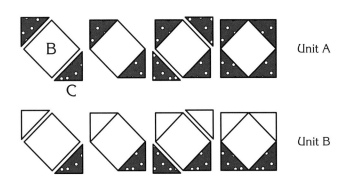

Unit A

Unit B

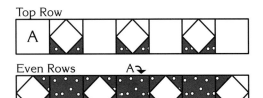

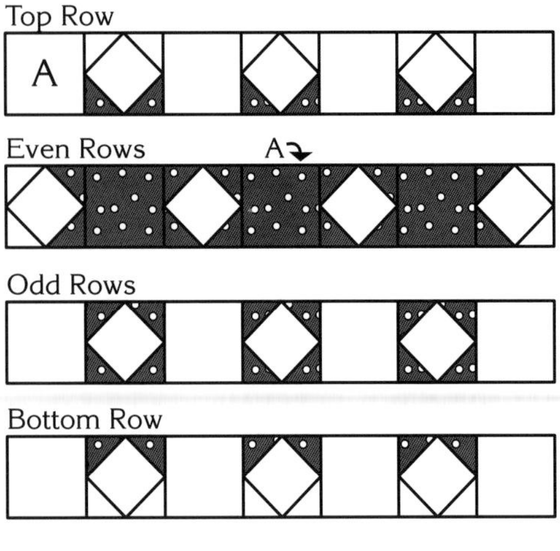

Top Row

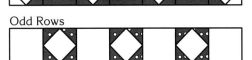

Even Rows

Odd Rows

Bottom Row

DIRECTIONS

Use ¼″ seam allowance throughout.

1. For CRIB size quilt, make 17 Unit A and 14 Unit B. For LITTLE quilt: 7 Unit A and 10 Unit B. For TWIN quilt: 67 Unit A and 26 Unit B.
2. Arrange A and B units in rows with background squares and star center squares. Unit A is used in the center of the quilt, and Unit B goes around the outside. See diagrams.
3. Stitch blocks into rows.
4. Stitch rows together. Press.
5. Refer to *Finishing Steps for All Quilts*, page 13. The blue quilt in the photo is outline quilted by hand; a one-inch grid is quilted in the center of each star; the four-heart pattern is quilted in the large background squares; and one heart is quilted in each small background square. The pink quilt in the photo is machine quilted in the background with loops and in the stars with outline quilting.

P.S. I Love You

PS I LOVE YOU

BLOCK SIZE: 3″

Use 42-44″ wide fabric. Photo is of the CRIB size quilt.

When strips appear in the cutting list, cut crossgrain strips (selvage to selvage).

Patterns for making templates, if you wish to use them, are on pages 70-73.

	Little	Crib	Twin
Approx. Finished Size	31x37″	45x57″	63x99″
Blocks Set	7x9	11x13	17x25
Total # of Blocks	63	143	425
	32 9-patch	72 9-patch	213 9-patch
	31 plain	71 plain	212 plain

YARDAGE

	Little	Crib	Twin
background & border	1¼ yds.	2¾ yds.	5¾ yds.
colored scraps to total	¾ yd.	1¼ yds.	2½ yds.
binding	⅜ yd.	½ yd.	¾ yd.
backing	1⅛ yds.	3 yds. H	6 yds. V
batting	35x41″	49x61″	67x103″

CUTTING	Pattern or Cut Size	Little	Crib	Twin
border	5½″ strip	4		
	*6½x57½″		2	
	*6½x33½″		1	
	*12½x33½″		1	
	*6½x99½″			2
	*6½x51½″			1
	*18½x51½″			1
background	A–3½″ square	31	71	212
	B–1½″ square	128	288	852
9-patch scraps	B–1½″ square	160	360	1065
girl/boy & letters**	pgs. 70-73		1 set	1 set
hearts	pg. 73	***	6 large	***
			75 others	
binding	2½″ strip	4	6	9

*Cut these borders on the lengthwise grain, then cut squares for blocks from the remaining fabric. Border lengths will need to be adjusted to *your* quilt (they will probably need to be shortened a bit).

**Letters are included for IT'S A BOY and IT'S A GIRL as well as PS I LOVE YOU.

***Use only hearts for the LITTLE quilt. For the TWIN quilt, cut any number of hearts of any size, depending on how far down the sides of the quilt you want them.

DIRECTIONS

Use ¼″ seam allowance throughout.

1. Make nine-patch blocks.
2. Arrange blocks in rows as shown.
3. Stitch blocks into rows.
4. Stitch rows together. Press.
5. Referring to *Stairstep Borders*, page 8, stitch top and bottom borders to quilt. Stitch side borders to quilt.
6. Applique girl or boy, letters, and hearts to border. On the TWIN quilt, the girl/boy should be placed near the bottom edge of the border, close to the block section of the quilt, so it will be centered on the pillow when the bed is made.
7. Refer to *Finishing Steps for All Quilts*, page 13. Quilt in photo is machine quilted in diagonals through the corners of the large background squares to the outer edges of the quilt, skipping over the appliques.

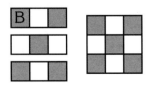

Odd Rows

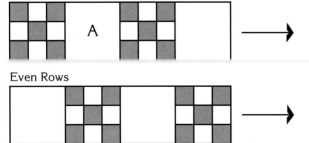

Even Rows

Tumbling Blocks

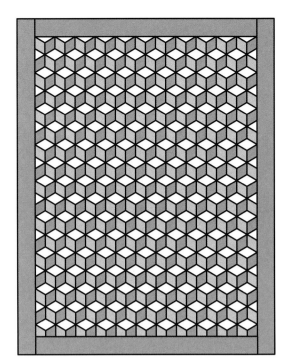

DIAMOND SIZE: 2″

Use 42-44″ wide fabric. Photo is of the CRIB size quilt. Other quilt in photo is *I Spy Napping Quilt*, directions on page 26. When strips appear in the cutting list, cut crossgrain strips (selvage to selvage). Pattern on page 64.

	Little	Crib	Twin
Approx. Finished Size	30x38″	44x56″	71x102″
Blocks Set	11 rows	17 rows	29 rows
Total # of Blocks	82	195	478

YARDAGE

	Little	Crib	Twin
lights to total	⅝ yd.	1⅛ yds.	2⅜ yds.
mediums to total	⅝ yd.	1⅛ yds.	2⅜ yds.
darks to total	⅝ yd.	1⅛ yds.	2⅜ yds.
border	½ yd.	⅝ yd.	2⅛ yds.
binding	⅜ yd.	½ yd.	¾ yd.
backing	1¼ yds.	3 yds. H	6⅛ yds. V
batting	35x43″	49x61″	71x106″

CUTTING

	Pattern or Cut Size	Little	Crib	Twin
lights	A–pg. 64	82	195	478
mediums	A–pg. 64	82	195	478
darks	A–pg. 64	82	195	478
border	3½″ strip	4	5	
	8½″ strip			8
binding	2½″ strip	4	6	9

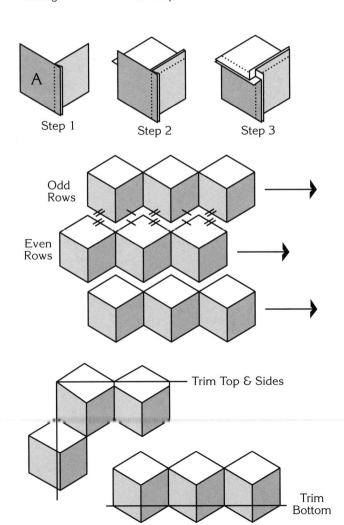

Step 1

Step 2

Step 3

Odd Rows

Even Rows

Trim Top & Sides

Trim Bottom

DIRECTIONS

Use ¼″ seam allowance throughout.

1. Make blocks, referring to diagram. Step 1 is an edge-to-edge seam. Steps 2 and 3 are stitched outer edge to center seam intersection and then backstitched.
2. Press seams of each block in a spiral.
3. Stitch rows of blocks with edge-to-edge seams. LITTLE: 6 rows of 7 blocks (odd rows), 5 rows of 8 (even rows). CRIB: 9 rows of 11 blocks (odd), 8 rows of 12 (even). TWIN: 15 rows of 16 blocks (odd), 14 rows of 17 (even). Do not press.
4. Stitch rows together: Pin each "uphill" segment to the next row (marked by one slash between first two rows in diagram). Stitch each segment separately, backstitching at each end of the short 2″ seam. Unpin as you sew. Pin and stitch all "downhill" segments in the same row in the same manner (double slashes in diagram). Press all row seams toward bottom of quilt.
5. Trim all four sides to straighten edges. See diagram.
6. See *Stairstep Borders*, page 8, for adding border. Top and bottom borders are stitched on first, then side borders.
7. Refer to *Finishing Steps for All Quilts*, page 13. Quilt in photo is outline quilted by hand in every diamond.

I Spy Napping Quilt

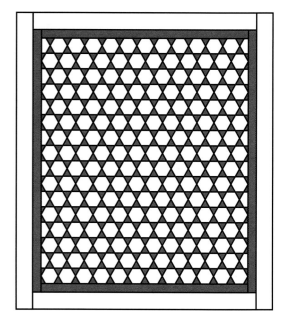

ROW HEIGHT APPROXIMATELY 2¾″

Dark version of quilt has "conversation" prints in the hexagons so children can play "I Spy". Photo of light version of quilt is on page 24.

Use 42-44″ wide fabric. When strips appear in the cutting list, cut crossgrain strips (selvage to selvage). Patterns on page 61.

Approx. Finished Size	46x53″
Setting	16 rows, 8 odd & 8 even

YARDAGE	Crib
hexagons–muslin for light quilt	2¼ yds.
scraps of "conversation" fabrics for dark quilt at least 4″ square to total	2 yds.
triangles–solid for dark quilt	1 yd.
bright pastel scraps for light quilt at least 3″ square to total	1 yd.
border 1	⅜ yd.
border 2	⅔ yd.
binding	½ yd.
backing	3⅛ yds. H
batting	51x57″

CUTTING	Pattern or Cut Size	Crib
hexagons	A–pg. 61	200
triangles	B–pg. 61	400
border 1	2″ strip	5
border 2	3½″ strip	6
binding	2½″ strip	6

Odd Rows

Even Rows

Trim

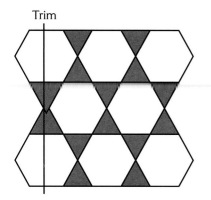

DIRECTIONS

Use ¼″ seam allowance throughout.

1. Make rows, referring to diagram. Odd rows have 13 hexagons and begin and end with hexagons. Even rows have 12 hexagons and begin and end with triangles.
2. Press all seams in odd rows to the right and all seams in even rows to the left.
3. Stitch rows together. Press well.
4. Trim sides to straighten edges. See diagram.
5. See *Stairstep Borders*, page 8, for adding borders. Top and bottom borders are stitched on first, then side borders.
6. On the inside border of the I Spy quilt, hand or machine embroider the names of items children can find in the hexagons.
7. Refer to *Finishing Steps for All Quilts*, page 13. Both quilts are quilted by machine in the ditch between all patches, and extra quilting lines are added in the second border of the light quilt.

Tiddly-Winks

BLOCK SIZE: 6″

Use 42-44″ wide fabric. Photo is of the CRIB size quilt.

When strips appear in the cutting list, cut crossgrain strips (selvage to selvage).

Patterns for making templates, if you wish to use them, are on page 62.

	Little	Crib	Twin
Approx. Finished Size	30x42″	42x54″	66x102″
Blocks Set	5x7	7x9	11x17
Total # of Blocks	35	63	187
	17 9-patch	31 9-patch	93 9-patch
	18 pinwh.	32 pinwh.	94 pinwh.

YARDAGE

	Little	Crib	Twin
background (both blocks)	⅞ yd.	1½ yds.	4 yds.
pinwheel fabric	⅝ yd.	⅞ yd.	2¼ yds.
nine-patch fabric	½ yd.	⅞ yd.	2¼ yds.
five or more brights for applique & binding*	¼ yd. ea.	¼ yd. ea.	
seven or more brights for applique & binding*			¼ yd. ea.
backing	1⅜ yds.	2⅞ yds. H	6⅛ yds. V
batting	34x46″	46x58″	70x106″

CUTTING

CUTTING	Pattern or Cut Size	Little	Crib	Twin
background	A–3⅞″ square**	36	64	188
	B–2½″ square	68	124	372
pinwheel fabric	A–3⅞″ square**	36	64	188
nine-patch fabric	B–2½″ square	85	155	465
applique circles	C–pg. 62	25	50	150
binding	2½″ strip***	15	20	34

*You will have extra.

**Cut these squares in half diagonally to make triangles.

***Vary the lengths of these 2½″ strips from 9″ to 13″.

DIRECTIONS

Use ¼″ seam allowance throughout.

1. Make nine-patch and pinwheel blocks following diagrams.
2. Arrange in rows as shown.
3. Stitch blocks into rows.
4. Stitch rows together.
5. Applique circles at random on both blocks.
6. Stitch binding strips together end to end, alternating colors.
7. Refer to *Finishing Steps for All Quilts*, page 13. Quilt in photo is machine quilted diagonally through centers of all blocks.

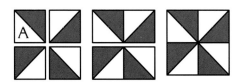

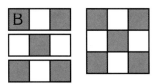

Odd Rows

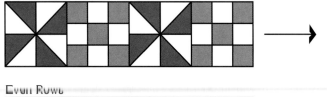

Even Rows

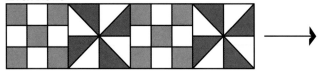

Bye Baby Bunting

SQUARE SIZE: 3″

This nap-sized quilt folds into its own pillow cover. Use 42-44″ wide fabric. When strips appear in the cutting list, cut crossgrain strips (selvage to selvage). Pattern for making a template, if you wish to use one, is on page 63.

Approx. Finished Size	42x57″ quilt & 18″ pillow
Squares Set	14x19 for quilt & 6x12 for pillow
Total # of Squares	266 for quilt & 72 for pillow

YARDAGE

flannel scraps for top to total	3¼ yds.
binding	½ yd.
backing for quilt & pillow cover	3⅜ yds.
pillow lining	⅝ yd.
batting	46x61″ for quilt, 22x40″ for pillow cover

CUTTING	Pattern or Cut Size	Number
squares	A–3½″ square	266 for quilt, 72 for pillow cover
binding	2½″ strip	5

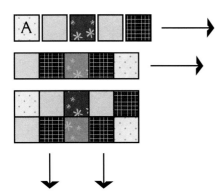

See page 48 for remaining diagrams.

DIRECTIONS

Use ¼″ seam allowance throughout.

1. Quilt: Stitch 19 rows of 14 squares. Stitch rows together. Refer to Steps 1-5 of *Finishing Steps for All Quilts*, page 13. Quilt in the ditch between squares. Cut backing and batting even with quilt top. Do not bind quilt yet.

2. Pillow: Stitch 6 rows of 12 squares. Stitch rows together. Press. Layer and quilt in the ditch between squares. Trim backing and batting even with top. See page 47 for remaining diagrams.

3. Cut a lining piece for the pillow cover by using the quilted piece for a pattern.

4. Lay pillow lining and quilted pillow cover piece right sides together. Stitch one long edge with ¼″ seam. Open out, press.

5. Fold in half crosswise, right sides together. Sew into tube with ¼″ seam.

6. Turn lining down over quilted piece, matching raw edges.

7. Center pillow cover on one end of back side of quilt, raw edges together. Baste.

8. Bind quilt, covering raw edges of pillow cover at the same time.

9. When you want to fold quilt into its attached pillow cover, lay quilt right side up and fold sides of quilt in, even with pillow cover. Fold three times, working toward pillow cover end of quilt. Turn cover to right side over folded quilt.

Simple Gifts

BLOCK SIZE: 6″
Use 42-44″ wide fabric. Photo is of the CRIB size quilt.
When strips appear in the cutting list, cut crossgrain strips (selvage to selvage).
Patterns for making templates, if you wish to use them, are on page 60.

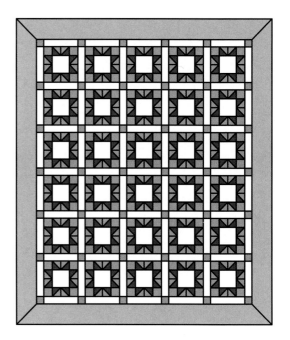

	Little	Crib	Twin
Approx. Finished Size	28x35″	44x51″	66x102″
Blocks Set	3x4	5x6	8x13
Total # of Blocks	12	30	104

YARDAGE

	Little	Crib	Twin
star background	⅝ yd.	1 yd.	3¼ yds.
star centers	¼ yd.	⅜ yd.	1¼ yds.
star points	⅓ yd.	⅔ yd.	2 yds.
sashing setting squares	⅛ yd.	⅙ yd.	⅜ yd.
sashing rectangles	⅜ yd.	¾ yd.	2⅛ yds.
border–if lengthwise stripe	1¼ yds.	1¾ yds.	3⅛ yds.
border–if not a stripe	½ yd.	¾ yd.	1⅛ yds.
binding	⅜ yd.	½ yd.	¾ yd.
backing	1 yd.	3 yds. H	6¼ yds. V
batting	32x40″	49x56″	71x107″

CUTTING

CUTTING	Pattern or Cut Size	Little	Crib	Twin
star background	A–2″ square	48	120	416
	B–2⅜″ square*	48	120	416
star centers	C–3½″ square	12	30	104
star points	B–2⅜″ square*	48	120	416
sashing setting sqs	D–1¾″ square	20	42	126
sashing rectangles	E–1¾x6½″	31	71	229
border if stripe	3x32″	2		
	3x40″	2		
	4x49″		2	
	4x56″		2	
	4x71″			2
	4x107″			2
border if not stripe	3″ strip	4		
	4″ strip		6	9
binding	2½″ strip	4	6	9

*Cut these squares in half diagonally to make triangles.

DIRECTIONS

Use ¼″ seam allowance throughout.
1. Make blocks following diagram.
2. To join blocks with sashing, see *Sashing With Corner Setting Squares*, page 8.
3. See *Mitered Borders*, page 8, for adding border.
4. Refer to *Finishing Steps for All Quilts*, page 13. Quilt in photo is machine quilted in the ditch between blocks and sashing strips, and around stars. Center squares of blocks are outline quilted, and border is quilted in several lines following stripe in fabric.

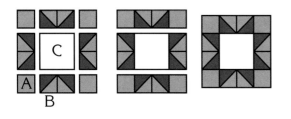

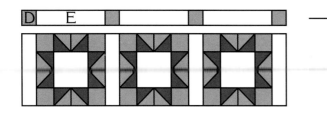

Pinwheels

BLOCK SIZE: 6″

Use 42-44″ wide fabric. Photo is of the CRIB size quilt. When strips appear in the cutting list, cut crossgrain strips (selvage to selvage). Patterns for quarter-block unit for paper piecing method and heart for quilting are on page 60.

	Little	Crib	Twin
Approx. Finished Size	26x32″	42x54″	66x102″
Blocks Set	3x4	5x7	9x15
Total # of Blocks	12	35	135

YARDAGE

	Little	Crib	Twin
pinwheel background–scraps at least 2¼x4½″ to total	⅞ yd.	2¼ yds.	8¾ yds.
pinwheels–scraps at least 4″ square to total	¾ yd.	1¾ yds.	6¼ yds.
border 1	½ yd.	⅓ yd.	½ yd.
border 2		1 yd.	1½ yds.
binding	⅜ yd.	½ yd.	¾ yd.
backing	1 yd.	2⅞ yds. H	6⅛ yds. V
batting	28x34″	46x58″	70x106″

CUTTING

	Pattern or Cut Size	Little	Crib	Twin
pinwheel background	2¼x4½″	96	280	1080
pinwheels	4″ square	48	140	540
border 1	1½″ strip	4	5	8
border 2	3½″ strip	4		
	5½″ strip		5	9
binding	2½″ strip	4	5	9

DIRECTIONS

The following directions are for the paper piecing method. If you prefer to make templates for traditional piecing, simply add seam allowance to the two triangle shapes in the quarter-block unit (pattern on page 60) and remember to cut half of the side triangles in reverse. Use ¼″ seam allowance throughout.

1. Make photocopies of the quarter block unit on page 60 to equal four times the number of blocks in the quilt you are making. Cut out each quarter-block pattern on outside line.
2. Lay one quarter-block pattern on table right side down. *Center* a 4x4″ piece of pinwheel fabric over it, right side up. *Center* (end to end) a 2¼x4½″ piece of background fabric right side down over the pinwheel fabric and hold the three layers up to the light. Slide the edge of the background fabric piece ¼″ past the seamline.
3. Turn the stack over, so paper side is up, and stitch on the line, extending the stitching line to the cut edges of the fabric. Use a very short stitch length to make removing paper easier.
4. Finger press background piece open and check to see that fabric covers paper pattern. Flip background piece back and trim both fabrics to a ¼″ seam allowance. Repeat on other side of unit. Trim fabric even with paper pattern.

Continued on page 48.

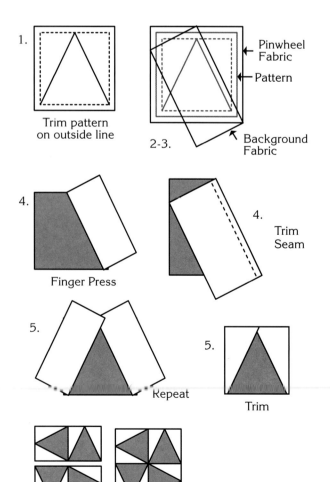

1. Trim pattern on outside line

2-3. Pinwheel Fabric / Pattern / Background Fabric

4. Finger Press

4. Trim Seam

5. Repeat

5. Trim

Rock-a-Bye

BLOCK SIZE: 6″

Use 42-44″ wide fabric. Photo is of the CRIB size quilt.
Patterns for making templates, if you wish to use them, are on page 69.

	Little	Crib	Twin
Approx. Finished Size	24x30″	42x54″	66x102″
Blocks Set	4x5	7x9	11x17
Total # of Blocks	20	63	187

YARDAGE

	Little	Crib	Twin
star background–scraps at least 4½″ square to total	¾ yd.	1⅞ yds.	4⅞ yds.
stars–scraps at least 4″ square to total	¾ yd.	1⅞ yds.	5⅛ yds.
binding	½ yd.	¾ yd.	1 yd.
backing	1 yd.	2⅞ yds. H	6⅛ yds. V
batting	28x34″	46x58″	70x106″

CUTTING

	Pattern or Cut Size	Little	Crib	Twin
star background	A–2″ square	80	252	748
	B–4¼″ square*	20	63	187
stars	C–3½″ square	20	63	187
	D–2⅜″ square**	80	252	748
binding	2½″ strip	4	5	9

*Cut these squares in quarters diagonally (with an X) to make triangles.
**Cut these squares in half diagonally to make triangles.

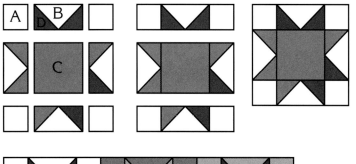

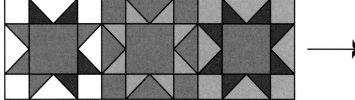

DIRECTIONS

Use ¼″ seam allowance throughout.

1. Make blocks following diagram, using a mixture of star scraps in each block.
2. Stitch rows together.
3. Stitch blocks into rows.
4. Refer to *Finishing Steps for All Quilts*, page 13. Quilt in photo is outline quilted by hand in all patches.

You Are My Sunshine

BLOCK SIZE: 7″

Use 42-44″ wide fabric. Photo is of the CRIB size quilt.
When strips appear in the cutting list, cut crossgrain strips (selvage to selvage).
Quilting pattern is on page 69.

		Little	Crib	Twin
Approx. Finished Size		21x35″	35x49″	63x105″
Blocks Set		3x5	5x7	9x15
Total # of Blocks		15	35	135
		8 A, 7 B	18 A, 17 B	68 A, 67 B

YARDAGE

		Little	Crib	Twin
background		⅞ yd.	1⅜ yds.	3½ yds.
fabric 1–center chain		½ yd.	¾ yd.	1⅞ yds.
fabric 2–middle chain		¾ yd.	1¼ yds.	3 yds.
fabric 3–outer chain		½ yd.	1 yd.	2¾ yds.
binding		⅔ yd.	⅞ yd.	1⅜ yds.
backing		⅞ yd.	1⅝ yds.	6⅜ yds. V
batting		25x39″	39x53″	67x109″

CUTTING

	Pattern or Cut Size	Little	Crib	Twin
background	5½″ strip	1	3	10
	3½″ strip	2	4	12
	1½″ strip	3	4	12
fabric 1–center chain	1½″ strip	7	13	39
fabric 2–middle chain	1½″ strip	13	24	66
fabric 3–outer chain	1½″ strip	11	20	60
binding	5″ strip	4	5	9

Block A   Block B

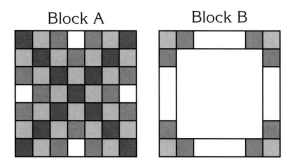

See page 49 for remaining diagrams.

DIRECTIONS

Use ¼″ seam allowance throughout.

1. Block A: Sew 1½″ strips together to make the four strip sets. For LITTLE QUILT: make one each of the four strip sets. For CRIB QUILT: make two each of Strip Sets 1-3 and one of Strip Set 4. For TWIN QUILT: make six each of Strip Sets 1-3 and three of Strip Set 4. Press seams in alternating directions as shown. Square up the end of each set and then cross-cut into 1½″ segments for rows. Arrange rows as shown to make blocks and stitch together. Press row seams in alternating directions as shown.

2. Block B: Make the two strip sets shown. For LITTLE QUILT: make one each. For CRIB QUILT: make two each. For TWIN QUILT: make six each. Press seams in both strip sets as shown. Cut both strip sets into 1½″ segments. Cut 5½″ background fabric strips into 5½″ squares. Stitch Row 5 to opposite sides of 5½″ squares. Press seams to *outside* of block. Stitch Row 6 to remaining sides of blocks. Press seams toward *center* of block.

3. Lay blocks out, alternating A and B, with A in each corner. Stitch blocks into rows.

4. Stitch rows together. Press well.

5. Refer to *Finishing Steps for All Quilts*, page 13, but do not trim away backing and batting after quilting. Refer to *One-Inch Binding*, page 12, for binding quilt. Quilt in photo is hand quilted through the middle chain, and a sun is quilted in the center of each Block B.

Facts of Life

Approx. Finished Size 28x36″
Use 42-44″ wide fabric.
When strips appear in the cutting list, cut crossgrain strips (selvage to selvage).
Patterns on pages 75-79.

YARDAGE

background	1 yd.
clouds	½ yd.
letters	½ yd. each of two colors
other appliques–scraps at least 6x8″ to total	1 yd.
binding	⅜ yd.
backing	1 yd.
batting	32x40″

CUTTING

	Pattern or Cut Size	Number
background	28x36″	
clouds	pgs. 77-78	3 large, 2 small
appliques	pgs. 75-79	5 flowers with leaves, 6 large stars, 1 ball, 1 boat, 1 duck, 1 rattle, 1 car, and letters as needed
binding	2½″ strip	4

DIRECTIONS

Use ¼″ seam allowance throughout.

1. Hand or machine applique pieces to background using photo and diagram as guides. Refer to *Quilting Techniques*, page 5.
2. Refer to *Finishing Steps for All Quilts*, page 13. Quilt in photo is machine quilted around each applique. Two extra lines of quilting are added around each cloud (⅝″ away and 1¼″ away).

Ring Around the Rosie

ROW WIDTH: 4¼"
Use 42-44" wide fabric.
When strips appear in the cutting list, cut crossgrain strips (selvage to selvage).
Patterns on page 61.

Approx. Finished Size 38x51"

YARDAGE

background	2 yds.
fabric 1–4-patches in **center** row	⅛ yd.
fabric 2–4-patches in rows **next to center**	¼ yd.
fabric 3–4-patches in "**border**" rows	⅜ yd.
hearts	¼ yd.
stems	⅛ yd.
leaves	⅛ yd.
binding	½ yd.
backing	2⅝ yds. H
batting	43x55"

CUTTING	Pattern or Cut Size	Number
background		
for applique rows	4¾x43"	4
for 4-patches	A–2" square	136
for small triangles	B–3" square*	14
for large triangles	C–5½" square**	31
fabric 1–4-patches	A–2" square	20
fabric 2–4-patches	A–2" square	40
fabric 3–4-patches	A–2" square	76
applique heart flowers	pg. 61	24
binding	2½" strip	5

*Cut these squares in *half* diagonally to make triangles.
**Cut these squares in *quarters* diagonally to make triangles.

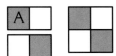

Make Four for Corners
with Fabric 3

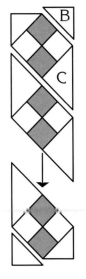
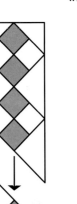
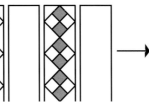

DIRECTIONS

Use ¼" seam allowance throughout.

1. Make 10 four-patches with Fabric 1 and background fabric, 20 four-patches with Fabric 2, and 34 four-patches with Fabric 3. Make four corner four-patches with Fabric 3 following diagram.

2. Assemble four-patch rows with large and small triangles. Vertical rows have 10 four-patches, and the two horizontal rows that finish the quilt have 9, including the corner four-patches. Check orientation of corner four-patches before stitching.

3. Applique six heart flowers to each background strip, spacing evenly, and alternating direction of stems. Note that the rows are all the same, but they are placed facing different directions.

4. Stitch vertical rows of four-patches and appliques together following diagram.

5. Stitch top and bottom horizontal rows of four-patches to quilt, making sure the corner four-patches are placed correctly.

6. Refer to *Finishing Steps for All Quilts*, page 13. Quilt in photo is machine quilted in the ditch between rows and around appliques.

Pick Up Sticks

BLOCK SIZE: 6¼″

Use 42-44″ wide fabric. Photo is of the CRIB size quilt. Other quilt in photo is *Facts of Life*, directions on page 40. We used a fabric with a sun motif for the center squares. When strips appear in the cutting list, cut crossgrain strips (selvage to selvage). Patterns for making templates, if you wish to use them, are on page 74.

	Little	Crib	Twin
Approx. Finished Size	24x36″	42x54″	64x101″
Blocks Set	3x5	5x7	8x14
Total # of Blocks	15	35	112

YARDAGE

	Little	Crib	Twin
center square fabric	⅛ yd.	¼ yd.	⅜ yd.
dark scraps from 2x2″ to 2x7″ to total	⅝ yd.	1¼ yds.	3⅛ yds.
light scraps from 2x2″ to 2x7″ to total	½ yd.	1 yd.	2⅜ yds.
border 1	½ yd.	⅓ yd.	¾ yd.
border 2		¾ yd.	1¼ yds.
binding	⅜ yd.	½ yd.	¾ yd.
backing	⅞ yd.	2⅞ yds. H	6⅛ yds. V
batting	28x40″	46x59″	68x106″

CUTTING

CUTTING	Pattern or Cut Size	Little	Crib	Twin
darks	A–1¾x1¾″	15	35	112
	B–1¾x3″	15	35	112
	C–1¾x4¼″	15	35	112
	D–1¾x5½″	15	35	112
	E–1¾x6¾″	15	35	112
lights	A–1¾x1¾″	15	35	112
	B–1¾x3″	15	35	112
	C–1¾x4¼″	15	35	112
	D–1¾x5½″	15	35	112
border 1 (little)	3″ strip	4		
border 1 (crib)	1¾″ strip		4	
border 2 (crib)	4½″ strip		5	
border 1 (twin)	3″ strip			8
border 2 (twin)	5″ strip			8
binding	2½″ strip	4	5	9

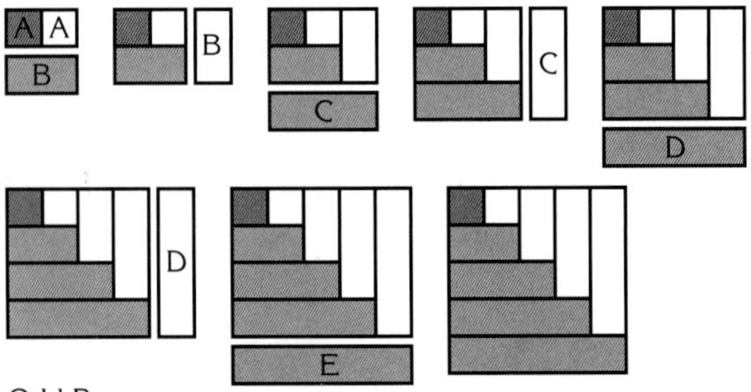

DIRECTIONS

Use ¼″ seam allowance throughout.

1. Make blocks following diagram.
2. Lay out rows of blocks, alternating position of lights and darks as shown. Odd rows begin with darks in lower left position, and even rows begin with lights in lower left position. Stitch blocks into rows.
3. Stitch rows together.
4. See *Stairstep Borders*, page 8, for adding borders. Top and bottom borders are stitched on first, then side borders.
5. Refer to *Finishing Steps for All Quilts*, page 13. Quilt in photo is machine quilted in the ditch between lights and darks and between borders.

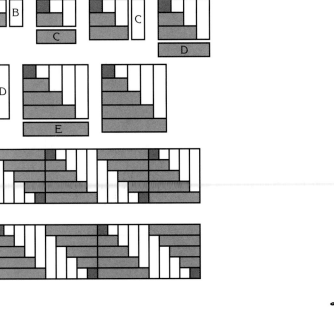

Odd Rows

Even Rows

Snips, Snails, & Puppy Dog Tails

Use 42-44″ wide fabric. When strips appear in the cutting list, cut crossgrain strips (selvage to selvage). Use ¼″ seam allowance throughout. Patterns for wall quilt are on pages 67-68.

CRIB QUILT – 42x42″

YARDAGE

dark, medium, & light homespuns	⅛ yd. each of 21 different fabrics
binding	½ yd.
backing	2⅞ yds. H
batting	46x46″

CUTTING

	Pattern or Cut Size	Number
homespuns	2½x42″	1 of each fabric
binding	2½″ strip	5

DIRECTIONS

1. Stitch long edges of strips together, grading from dark to light to dark, if desired.
2. Refer to *Finishing Steps for All Quilts*, page 13. Quilt in photo is machine quilted in the ditch between the strips.

WALL QUILT – 30x30″

YARDAGE

dog body, head	¼ yd.
dog ears, tail, feet	⅛ yd.
dog nose, eyes	tiny scraps
scarf	⅙ yd.
butterfly	scraps at least 2x4″
upper background	½ yd.
lower background	¼ yd.
border 1	⅙ yd.
border 2	⅜ yd.
border 3	½ yd.
binding	⅜ yd.
backing	1 yd.
batting	34x34″

CUTTING

	Pattern or Cut Size	Number
dog & butterfly	pgs. 67-68	1 set
upper background	12½x18½″	1
lower background	6½x18½″	1
border 1	1½″ strip	4
border 2	2½″ strip	4
border 3	3½″ strip	4
binding	2½″ strip	4

DIRECTIONS

1. Stitch upper and lower background pieces together.
2. Applique dog and butterfly to background using photo and diagram as guides.
3. Embroider legs and mouth with a stem stitch and the butterfly path with a running stitch.
4. See *Stairstep Borders*, page 8, for adding borders. Top and bottom borders are stitched on first, then side borders.
5. Refer to *Finishing Steps for All Quilts*, page 13. Background of quilt in photo is machine quilted diagonally in 2″ squares, and the dog and butterfly are ¼″ outline quilted.

JACKS
Continued from page 16.

half-blocks together, aligning four triangle points in the center. Finger press seams to spread out the bulk of the seam allowance as much as possible. Stitch; press seams. Repeat for remaining blocks.

3. To join blocks with sashing, see *Sashing With No Setting Squares*, page 8.

4. See *Stairstep Borders*, page 8, for adding first border. Side borders are stitched on first, then top and bottom.

5. Place remaining triangles on Border 1, right sides together and raw edges even, spreading or tucking one inside the next as needed to make them fit. LITTLE quilt has 9 on each end and 11 on each side. CRIB quilt has 14 on each end and 17 on each side. TWIN quilt has 21 on each end and 31 on each side. Pin well and then baste in place.

6. Add second border. Press seam to inside of quilt, allowing border triangles to point to outside of quilt.

7. Refer to *Finishing Steps for All Quilts*, page 13. Quilt in photo is machine quilted in the ditch between blocks and sashing and between borders.

PINWHEELS
Continued from page 34.

5. Repeat for the other three quarter-block units. Stitch units together to make one block, referring to diagram. Remove paper.

6. Repeat for required number of blocks.

7. Stitch blocks into rows.

8. Stitch rows together.

9. See *Stairstep Borders*, page 8, for adding borders. Top and bottom borders are stitched on first, then side borders.

10. Refer to *Finishing Steps for All Quilts*, page 13. Quilt in photo is machine quilted in the ditch at block and quarter-block seams. Hearts are hand quilted in the border, all positioned with the points toward the bottom of the quilt.

BYE BABY BUNTING
Continued from page 30.

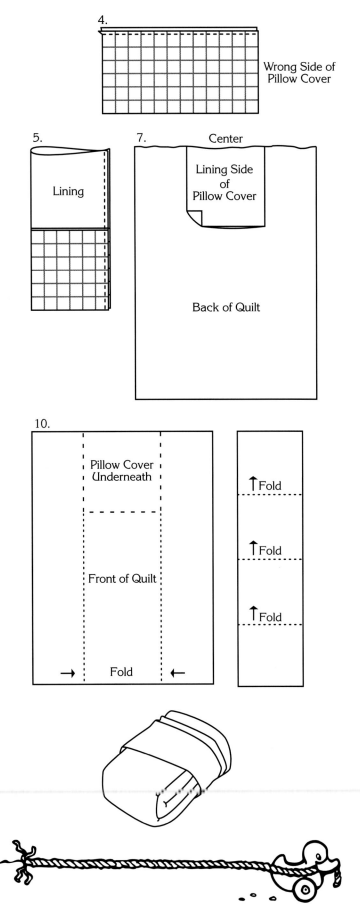

4.

Wrong Side of Pillow Cover

5.

Lining

7.

Center

Lining Side of Pillow Cover

Back of Quilt

10.

Pillow Cover Underneath

Front of Quilt

Fold

↑ Fold

↑ Fold

↑ Fold

YOU ARE MY SUNSHINE

Continued from page 38.

1. TO MAKE BLOCK A

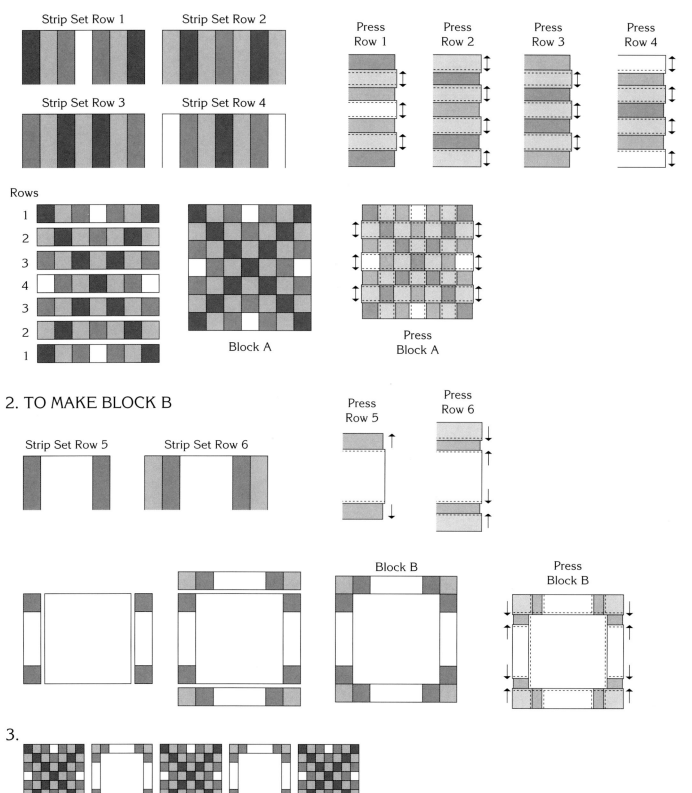

Strip Set Row 1   Strip Set Row 2

Strip Set Row 3   Strip Set Row 4

Press Row 1   Press Row 2   Press Row 3   Press Row 4

Rows

1
2
3
4
3
2
1

Block A

Press Block A

2. TO MAKE BLOCK B

Strip Set Row 5   Strip Set Row 6

Press Row 5   Press Row 6

Block B

Press Block B

3.

Accessories

We have designed several accessories to make your special quilt even more fun. Complete your crib ensemble with sheets, bumper pads, and a dust ruffle. You can even make a chair seat pad and chair back for a rocker. The new mother will be most appreciative. Find these and other great projects in this section. Several of the stuffed dolls, bears, and bunnies featured in the photos are patterns available from *Possibilities*®. See page 57 for details.

Crib Sheet

Pictured on page 45.
To fit a standard crib mattress—27x52″.

YARDAGE & SUPPLIES
2 yds. fabric (44″ wide)
1 yd. ¼″ elastic
4½ yds. ½″ wide single-fold bias tape (optional)
matching thread

DIRECTIONS
Use ¼″ seam allowance throughout.
1. Cut a 43x68″ rectangle from fabric.
2. Cut out an 8″ square from each corner. See diagram on page 51.
3. With right sides together, pin edge "A" to edge "B" at each corner. Stitch with a ¼″ seam allowance.
4. Bind or hem raw edges:
   To bind edges using bias tape: Fold bias tape in half lengthwise and press. Slip folded edge over raw edge of sheet and pin. Machine stitch bias tape using a straight stitch or a small zigzag.
   Stitched hem: Press a ¼″ double hem to wrong side. Stitch next to fold.
5. Pin the center of a 9″ piece of elastic to the wrong side of each sheet corner with the edge of the elastic about ⅛″ from bias tape or hemmed edge. Machine stitch from this center point along elastic with a zigzag stitch, stretching elastic as tight as possible. Start from center and stitch to end of elastic. Repeat for other end of elastic. Repeat for other three corners.

Bumper Pads

Pictured on page 45.
To fit a standard crib (mattress 27x52″). Six units with finished measurements of approximately 10x26″ each. See optional arched headboard on page 52.

YARDAGE & SUPPLIES
3¼ yds. fabric (42-44″ wide) for 6 bumpers (4 yds. if fabric is directional on the lengthwise grain)
⅜ yd. fabric (42-44″ wide) for cording
2¼ yds. 48″ wide/6 oz. batting
4⅞ yds. size #150 cording
1″ thick foam—enough to cut six pieces 8½x24½″
matching thread

CUTTING
12 pieces of fabric for bumpers 11½x27″
6 pieces of fabric for cording 1½x28″
24 pieces of fabric for ties 1½x14″
6 pieces of batting 19x24½″
6 pieces of cording 28″ long
6 pieces of foam 8½x24½″

DIRECTIONS
Use ¼″ seam allowance throughout.
1. Lay cording along center of wrong side of 1½x28″ pieces of fabric. Fold fabric over cording, aligning raw edges. Using a zipper foot and a medium stitch length, baste with matching thread. Sew close to cord but not too close. Repeat for remaining five cording pieces.

2. With right sides together and raw edges even, machine baste each cording piece to one long edge of each of the bumper pad fronts. Sew on the same stitching line as before.

3. Press in ¼″ on long edges of tie pieces. Fold in half lengthwise and edgestitch, turning in seam allowance on one short end. Repeat for other 23 ties. Pin ties, with raw edges even, to the short ends of the six bumper pad fronts. Pin them 1″ from top edges and 1½″ from bottom edges. Pin loose ends of ties down so they do not get caught while sewing.

4. Pin the back to each bumper pad. Stitch, starting at X and ending at Y. See diagram at right. Stitch as close to cording as possible. Leave bottom edge open for stuffing. Trim corners, turn right sides out, and press. Wrap batting around foam and stuff into bumper pads with folded edges of batting toward top edges of bumpers. Turn one seam allowance over the other and slipstitch closed by hand.

Dust Ruffle

Pictured on page 45.
To fit a standard crib (mattress 27x52″).

YARDAGE & SUPPLIES
4⅝ yds. fabric (42-44″ wide)
matching thread

CUTTING
Cut pieces following diagram at right.

DIRECTIONS
Use ¼″ seam allowance throughout.

1. Stitch one A and two B sections together for each side. Stitch one C and one D section together for each end.

2. Press ¼″ to wrong side on one long edge of each ruffle section. Press 2¼″ hem to wrong side and stitch in place.

3. Press ¼″ double hem to wrong side on the short end of each ruffle section. Stitch in place.

4. Sew two rows of gathering stitches on top edge of each ruffle section, ⅛″ apart and ½″ from raw edge.

5. Attach end ruffles to center panel: Pull gathering to 26″ and pin to panel, right sides together, leaving ½″ of center panel free at either end. Stitch with ½″ seam allowance.

6. Attach side ruffles: Pull gathering to 51″ and pin to panel, right sides together, folding under the ½″ extension of center panel seam allowance at each end. Stitch with ½″ seam allowance. Press seam allowances toward center panel. Optional: Topstitch seam to center panel.

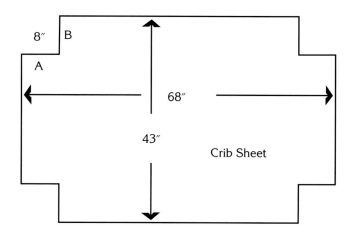

Crib Sheet

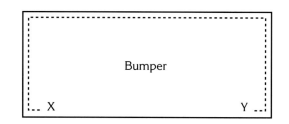

Bumper

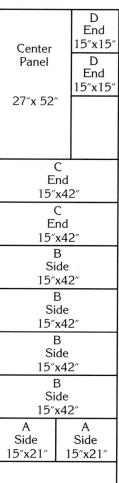

Dust Ruffle

Headboard

Pictured on page 45. Applique pattern on page 74.
To fit a standard crib (mattress 27x52″).

YARDAGE & SUPPLIES

1 yd. fabric (42-44″ wide)
⅜ yd. fabric for sun
¼ yd. fabric for face circle
⅛ yd. fabric for cording
1 yd. 48″ wide/6 oz. batting
1¾ yds. size #150 cording
1″ thick foam—18x28″
matching thread

Enlarge headboard drawing to make a pattern 28″ wide by 17″ high.

CUTTING

2 pieces of fabric using headboard pattern
1 piece of foam and two pieces of batting about 1″
    smaller than pattern all around
2 pieces of fabric for cording 1½x42″
4 pieces of fabric for ties 1½x14″
1 piece of cording 60″ long

DIRECTIONS

Use ¼″ seam allowance throughout.

1. Applique sun and face circle to center of one head-board fabric piece, referring to hand or machine applique directions, page 5, for preparing applique pieces. We used a contrasting thread for machine applique.

2. Stitch the 1½x42″ fabric pieces (for cording) together to make a piece 1½x84″. Trim to make piece 60″. Lay cording along center of wrong side of piece of fabric. Fold fabric over cording, aligning raw edges. Using a zipper foot and a medium stitch length, baste with matching thread. Sew close to cord, but not too close.

3. With right sides together and raw edges even, machine baste covered cording to curved edge of headboard. Sew on the same stitching line as before.

4. Press in ¼″ on long edge of tie pieces. Fold in half lengthwise and sew, turning in seam allowance on one short end. Repeat for other three ties. Pin ties 1½″ and 9½″ from bottom edge of headboard. Pin loose ends of ties down so they do not get caught while sewing.

5. Pin the back to headboard. Stitch, starting at X and ending at Y. See diagram at right. Stitch as close to cording as possible. Leave bottom edge open for stuffing. Trim corners, turn right side out. and press. Layer batting and foam pieces and insert into head-board. Turn one seam allowance over the other and slipstitch closed by hand.

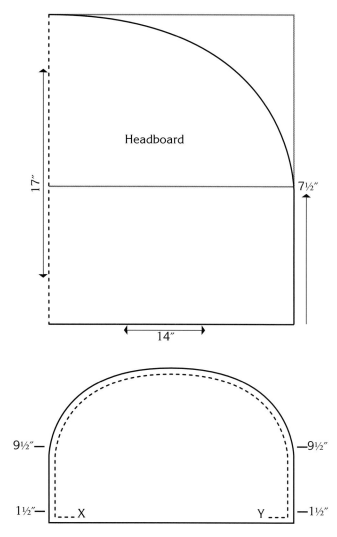

Simon Says Pillow

12″ square. Pictured on page 15. Pattern on page 62.

YARDAGE & SUPPLIES

9 fabric scraps at least 5″ square
½ yd. muslin
½ yd. fabric for pillow backing
14″ square of batting
12″ pillow form
matching thread

CUTTING

nine 4½″ squares (pattern piece A) from scraps
one 14″ square of muslin
two 12½″ squares for pillow backing

DIRECTIONS

Use ¼″ seam allowance throughout.

1. Stitch the squares together into a nine patch block as shown. Press.

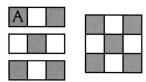

2. Place batting over muslin. Center pieced pillow top, right side up, over batting.
3. Machine quilt in the ditch and through the centers of all squares. Press. Trim batting and muslin even with nine-patch top.
4. Make envelope back: Press and then stitch a 4″ hem on one side of each 12½″ backing square. Lay pillow top right side up and place one backing piece, wrong side up and raw edges even, on top. Place other backing piece on top in the same manner, overlapping hems at center. Pin. Stitch around entire edge. Trim corners. Turn right side out. Press.

Overlap Backs on Pillow Top

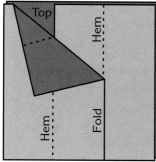

5. Insert pillow form into pillow cover through envelope back opening.

Receiving Blanket

41″ square. Pictured on page 21.

YARDAGE & SUPPLIES
2⅝ yds. flannel (42-44″ wide)
matching thread
3 skeins embroidery floss for blanket stitching & tying

DIRECTIONS
Use ¼″ seam allowance throughout.
1. Cut two 42″ squares.
2. Lay right sides together and stitch around outside edge, leaving an opening for turning.
3. Turn right side out. Press edges and make sure blanket is flat. Slipstitch opening closed.
4. Measure and mark a grid for tying. Using 6 strands of embroidery floss, and referring to *Tying a Quilt*, page 11, tie at marks.

5. Blanket stitch around edge.

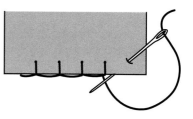

Note: Use the edge of a piece of tractor-feed computer paper to help keep stitches even. Place the strip with the holes in it even with the edge of the blanket and mark in each hole.

Jacks Pillow

9″ square. Pictured on page 17. Patterns on page 62.

YARDAGE & SUPPLIES
¼ yd. of fabric for background
¼ yd. of fabric for folded triangles
⅛ yd. of fabric for border
⅜ yd. of fabric for pillow backing
polyester fiberfill
matching thread

CUTTING
four 3½″ squares for background (pattern A)
four 3½″ squares for folded triangles (A)
two 2x6½″ rectangles for border (B)
two 2x9½″ rectangles for border
one 9½″ square for backing

DIRECTIONS
Use ¼″ seam allowance throughout.
1. To make folded triangle block, follow Steps 1-2 of *Jacks* quilt on page 16.
2. Stitch the 2x6½″ borders to the top and bottom of the block; stitch the 2x9½″ borders to the sides. Press.

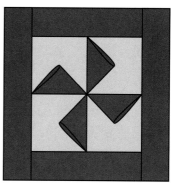

3. With right sides together, lay folded triangle block on pillow backing. Stitch around outside edge, leaving a 3″ opening on one side for turning.
4. Trim corners and turn right side out through opening. Press.
5. Stuff pillow with fiberfill to desired firmness.
6. Slipstitch opening closed.

Jacks Chair Seat Pad & Chair Back Cover

Chair Seat Pad 13″ square. Chair Back Cover 13x20″ (two identical sections are tied together). Pictured on page 17. Patterns on page 62.

YARDAGE & SUPPLIES
½ yd. fabric for background of blocks and borders
five fabric scraps at least 9″ square for folded triangles
¼ yd. fabric for sashing and binding
⅓ yd. fabric for chair back ties
1⅛ yds. for backing
1 yd. extra-loft batting
matching thread

CUTTING

block bkgrnd.	twenty 3½″ squares (pattern A)
folded triangles	twenty 3½″ squares (A) (4 per fabric)
sashing strips	eight 2x6½″ (B)
	two 2x9½″ (C) (chair seat)
	four 2x17″ (chair backs)
borders	six 2½x9½″
	two 2½x13½″
	four 2½x21″
backing	one 15″ square (chair seat)
	two 15x23″ pieces (chair backs)
binding	five 2½″ selvage-to-selvage strips
chair back ties	eight 3½x22″
batting	one 15″ square for chair seat
	two 15x23″ pieces for chair backs

CHAIR SEAT PAD DIRECTIONS
Use ¼″ seam allowance throughout.
1. Make one folded triangle block following Steps 1-2 of *Jacks* quilt on page 16. Pinwheels can spin in opposite directions by re-pressing triangles.
2. Stitch the 6½″ sashing strips to the top and bottom of the block. Stitch the 2x9½″ strips to the sides.
3. Stitch the 2½x9½″ border pieces to the top and bottom. Stitch the 2½x13½″ border pieces to the sides. Press.

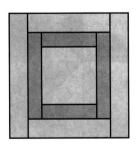

4. Lay batting on wrong side of chair seat backing. Center chair seat front on top of batting. Baste or pin together.
5. Machine quilt in the ditch between blocks and sashing and between borders.
6. Bind, referring to *Binding*, page 11.

CHAIR BACK COVER DIRECTIONS
Use ¼″ seam allowance throughout.
1. Make four folded triangle blocks following Steps 1-2 of *Jacks* quilt on page 16.
2. Join the blocks by adding the sashing. See diagram. Stitch borders to top and bottom first, then the sides.

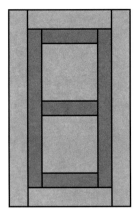

3. Lay batting on wrong side of backing fabric. Center chair backing front on top of batting. Baste or pin together. Repeat for other piece.
4. Machine quilt in the ditch between blocks and sashing and between borders.
5. Bind, referring to *Binding*, page 11.
6. Make ties by folding tie pieces lengthwise in half, right sides together. Stitch across one short end and up the long side. Clip corners and turn right side out. Press.
7. Hand stitch ties to all corners of chair back covers.

Color Forms Valance

Pictured on page 19. Applique patterns on pages 65-66. It is easy to customize this valance to fit any window. Measure window opening and multiply the measurement by two. Divide answer by 6. Round up.
For example:
window measurement = 50″
50″ x 2 = 100″
100″ ÷ 6 = 16.6
round up to 17
window needs 17 sections

YARDAGE & SUPPLIES
scraps of fabric at least 7x12″ for background
scraps of fabric at least 6x8″ for hearts
scraps of fabric at least 6x8″ for stars
scraps of fabric at least 6x8″ for moon
¼ yd. or more fabric for border, depending on size
1 yd. or more fabric for backing, depending on size

CUTTING

6½x11½″ rectangles for background
hearts, stars, and moons to applique to rectangles
3″x length of valance for border (piece as necessary)
14″x length of valance for backing (piece as necessary)

DIRECTIONS

Refer to hand or machine applique directions, page 5, for preparing applique pieces. Use ¼″ seam allowance throughout.

1. Applique hearts, stars, and moon to background rectangles, keeping shapes approximately ¾″ from bottom raw edge.
2. Stitch rectangles together to form a row. Press.
3. Measure valance, then cut border and backing.
4. Add border to bottom of row. Press.
5. With right sides together, lay appliqued row on top of backing. Stitch all around valance, leaving a 3″ opening on one end. Trim corners and turn right side out. Press.
6. Slipstitch opening closed. Lightly mark two lines, 1½″ and 3″ from top to form casing.
7. Stitch along these two lines.
8. At both ends, carefully slit the stitches between the 1½″ line and the 3″ line. A curtain rod will now easily slip into the casing.

P.S. I Love You Pillow

16″ square. Pictured on page 23. Patterns on pages 72-73.

YARDAGE & SUPPLIES

½ yd. fabric for background
fabric scraps at least 7″ square for boy
fabric scraps at least 3″ square for hearts
floral fabric scraps at least 1½x6½″ for cording
18″ square muslin
½ yd. fabric for backing
18″ square batting
16″ pillow form
2 yds. cording size #150
matching thread

CUTTING

16½″ square for background
boy and assorted hearts (use photo for color reference and heart sizes)
two 16½″ squares for backing
twelve 1½x6½″ fabric scraps for cording

DIRECTIONS

Refer to hand or machine applique directions, page 5, for preparing applique pieces. Use ¼″ seam allowance throughout.

1. Applique boy and hearts to background by hand or machine. We used the invisible open zigzag described in *Machine Applique* on pages 5-6.
2. Place batting on top of muslin. Center applique piece on top of batting.
3. Outline quilt around boy and hearts. Trim batting and muslin to match applique top.
4. Stitch fabric cording pieces end to end to make a strip about 72″ long.
5. Lay cording along the center on the wrong side of the 1½x72″ strip. Fold fabric over cording, aligning raw edges. Using a zipper foot, stitch close to the cording, but not too close.
6. Pin or machine baste cording to the right side of the applique pillow top with raw edges even. Overlap ends and gently curve cording around corners. Use zipper foot to stitch cording in place, making sure to stitch on previous machine stitching line.
7. Make envelope back: Press and then stitch a 4″ hem on one side of each 16½″ backing square. Lay pillow top right side up and place one backing piece, wrong side up and raw edges even, on top. Place other backing piece on top in the same manner, overlapping hems at center. Pin. Stitch around entire outside edge of pillow, using the zipper foot and stitching as close to the cording as possible.
8. Trim corners and turn pillow right side out. Press.
9. Insert pillow form into pillow cover through envelope back opening.

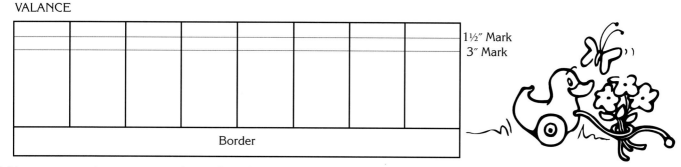

VALANCE

1½″ Mark
3″ Mark

Border

Add as many sections as you need to make valance two times the window measurement.

Simple Gifts Pillow

9″ square. Pictured on page 33. Patterns on page 60.

YARDAGE & SUPPLIES
scraps for star, background, & border
9½″ square muslin
¼ yd. fabric for backing
9½″ square of batting
polyester fiberfill – small amount
matching thread

CUTTING
four 2″ squares of background (pattern piece A)
four 2⅜″ squares of background cut in half
   diagonally(pattern piece B)
one 3½″ square (C) for star center
four 2⅜″ squares cut in half diagonally (B) for star
   points
four 1¾″ squares (D) for corner squares in border
four 1¾x6½″ rectangles (E) for border
one 9½″ square for pillow backing

DIRECTIONS
Use ¼″ seam allowance throughout.
1. Make block following diagram.

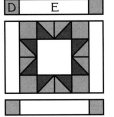
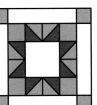
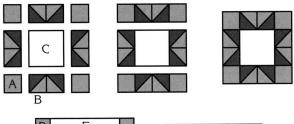

2. Lay batting on top of muslin. Center pieced block on
   top of batting. Machine quilt in the ditch around block
   and around star. Outline quilt center square. Trim all
   edges even with top.
3. With right sides together, lay quilted pillow top on
   backing. Stitch around outside edge, leaving a 3″
   opening for turning. Trim corners. Turn right side out.
   Press.
4. Stuff to desired firmness. Slipstitch opening closed.

Snips, Snails, & Puppy Dog Tails Pillow

12″ square. Pictured on page 47. Patterns on page 67-68.

YARDAGE & SUPPLIES

upper background	¼ yd.
lower background	¼ yd.
dog body, head	¼ yd.
dog ears, tail, feet	⅛ yd.
dog nose, eyes	tiny scraps
scarf	⅙ yd.
backing	⅜ yd.
pillow form	12″
matching thread	

CUTTING

upper background	6½x12½″
lower background	6½x12½″
dog	1 set of pieces
backing	two 12½″ squares

DIRECTIONS
Refer to hand or machine applique directions, page 5,
for preparing applique pieces. Use ¼″ seam allowance
throughout.
1. Stitch upper and lower background pieces right sides
   together to make 12½″ square.
2. Applique dog to background using photo and diagram as guides. We used the invisible open zigzag
   described in *Machine Applique* on pages 5-6.
3. Embroider legs and mouth with stem stitch.
4. Make envelope back: Press and then stitch a 4″ hem
   on one side of each 12½″ backing square. Lay pillow
   top right side up and place one backing piece, wrong
   side up and raw edges even, on top. Place other
   backing piece on top in the same manner, overlapping hems at center. Pin. Stitch around entire edge.
   Trim corners. Turn right side out. Press.
5. Insert pillow form into pillow cover through envelope
   back opening.

Covered Boxes

Boxes

Papier-mâché boxes are very popular and can be found in local craft stores. They are available in a wide variety of sizes and shapes, including squares, rectangles, hexagons, and hearts. Boxes from around home are also excellent for covering. Shoe, shirt/sweater, jewelry, and even oatmeal boxes will work.

Measuring Box & Figuring Yardage

Measure box as indicated in the following section and figure yardage based on these measurements. Figure yardage for each piece, adding extra for spacing the pieces apart from each other when drawing them on fusible web. If using the same fabric for more than one part, combine measurements. The example is based on a box 6″ high with a lid diameter of 10½″ and a lid depth of 1″. Round lid must have separate lid band.

LID TOP

Measure diameter of lid and add 1″.
For example: 10½″ lid top + 1″ = 11½″

11½″ Lid Top Piece

LID BAND

For length of lid band, measure circumference of lid and add ½″.
For example: 33″ lid circumference + ½″ = 33½″

For height of lid band, measure height of lid and add ½″.
For example: 1″ lid height + ½″ = 1½″

1½″ x 33½″ Lid Band Piece

SIDES

For depth of side piece, measure depth of box and add 1″.
For example: 6″ depth + 1″ = 7″
For length of side piece, measure circumference of box and add ½″.
For example: 32¼″ circumference + ½″ = 32¾″

7″ x 32¾″ Side Piece

Preparing Pattern Pieces For Fusing

Begin by reading the directions that come with your favorite brand of paper-backed fusible web. Follow these directions for iron temperature, length of time to press, and any other specific instructions. **Note:** For appliqued sun, enlarge or reduce the pattern on page 74 to fit your lid. Fuse to lid fabric and machine applique if desired.

1. Draw each piece on fusible web, leaving space between pieces for cutting. Label each piece.
2. Cut pieces apart between lines, leaving a margin of web outside all drawn lines.
3. Fuse to wrong side of fabric. Cut out on drawn lines.
4. Peel paper backing from pieces.

Fusing Fabric Pieces to Box

BOX SIDES

1. Wrap fusible side of fabric around side of box, overlapping ends and making sure there is an equal amount of excess fabric hanging over at top and bottom edges of box (approx. ½″). Fuse into place. Put the box over the point of the ironing board, turning it around as you iron and fuse.
2. Rest side of box on top of ironing board. Fold fabric to inside along top edge. Fuse into place with point of iron.
3. Set box on ironing board, bottom side up. Gently pull fabric over edge of box to bottom, easing and fusing.

LID

1. Center fused fabric on top of lid, making sure that excess fabric is even all the way around. Press and fuse into place.
2. Stand lid on edge of ironing board and gently stretch fabric over top edge, easing and fusing to lid band.

LID BAND

1. To apply strip to lid band, put one straight edge along top edge of lid and fuse smoothly into place, overlapping ends.
2. Stand lid on edge of ironing board and gently pull fabric over edge to inside of lid. Fuse.

Finishing Boxes

To personalize boxes, add penstitching, lettering, appliques, buttons, charms, trims, and embellishments of choice.

More Ideas

For over 50 more box ideas and patterns, order our book *Simply Fuse & Use*. See below.

Quilt Labels

With minimum effort, you can personalize your *P.S. I Love You Two* quilts. The label can be attached to the front or the back of the quilt, and it can provide a "secret pocket" for including extra tidbits of love. The tiny, tucked-in treasures could be items of special significance to the recipient such as a special letter. They could be scraps of fabric that in years to come could be used for patching or repairing the quilt, should the need arise. The label is a reminder of the warm thoughts that were inspiration for making the quilt in the first place. You can penstitch a label or embroider it. Penstitching is "stitching with a pen". It looks like hand stitching but is done with a permanent marking pen rather than needle and thread. It is quick, easy, and fun to do.

SUPPLIES

8″ square of muslin or solid light-colored fabric
8″ square of freezer paper
black or brown fine-point permanent marking pen
colored permanent marking pens to match quilt

TO PENSTITCH A QUILT LABEL

1. Prewash the fabric to be used for the label. Press. Sizing in the fabric may resist the ink or cause it to bleed. To make the fabric more stable for tracing, iron a piece of freezer paper to the wrong side of the fabric. Leave the paper on until the penstitching and coloring are finished.
2. Make a copy of the quilt label.
3. Tape the paper pattern to a window with good sunlight and then tape the fabric over the pattern.
4. Trace the design using a fine-point black or brown permanent marking pen.
5. Fill in the blanks with personal information using the same pen. Be sure to include the name of the quilt maker and the date.
6. Use permanent colored marking pens to color the motifs or design as desired.
7. Remove freezer paper and cut label out along dotted line. Press under ¼″ along all edges.
8. Slipstitch to quilt.

Optional: If you would prefer to embroider the label, transfer design to fabric as above, remove freezer paper, and embroider with desired threads.

Especially For

An Original From P.S. I Love You Two by Possibilities®

An Original From P.S. I Love You Two by Possibilities®

An Original From P.S. I Love You Two by Possibilities®

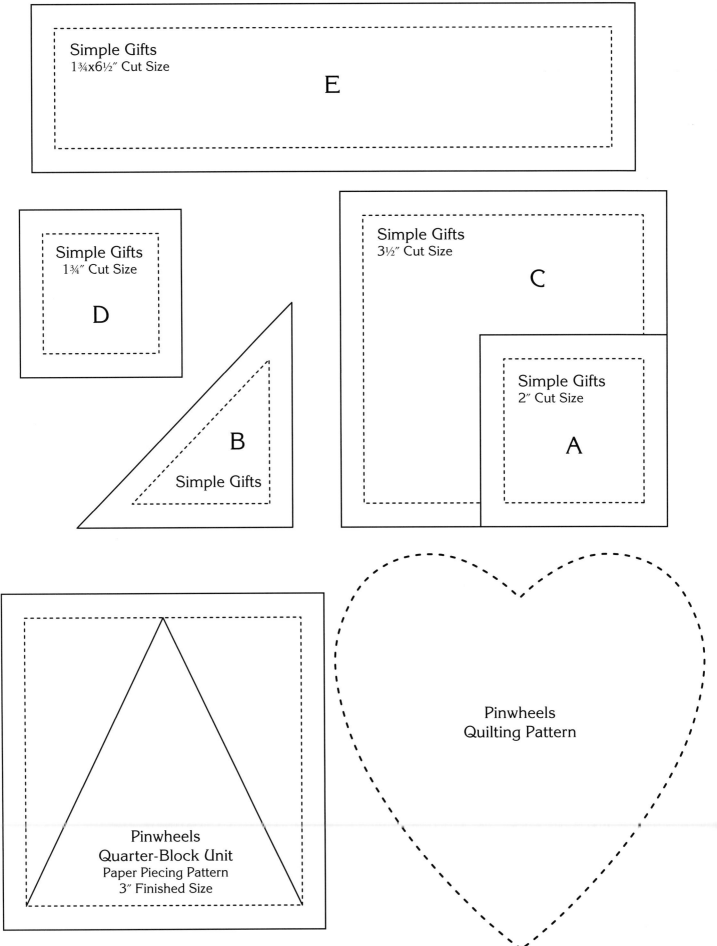

Simple Gifts
1¾x6½″ Cut Size

E

Simple Gifts
1¾″ Cut Size

D

Simple Gifts
3½″ Cut Size

C

Simple Gifts
2″ Cut Size

A

B

Simple Gifts

Pinwheels
Quarter-Block Unit
Paper Piecing Pattern
3″ Finished Size

Pinwheels
Quilting Pattern

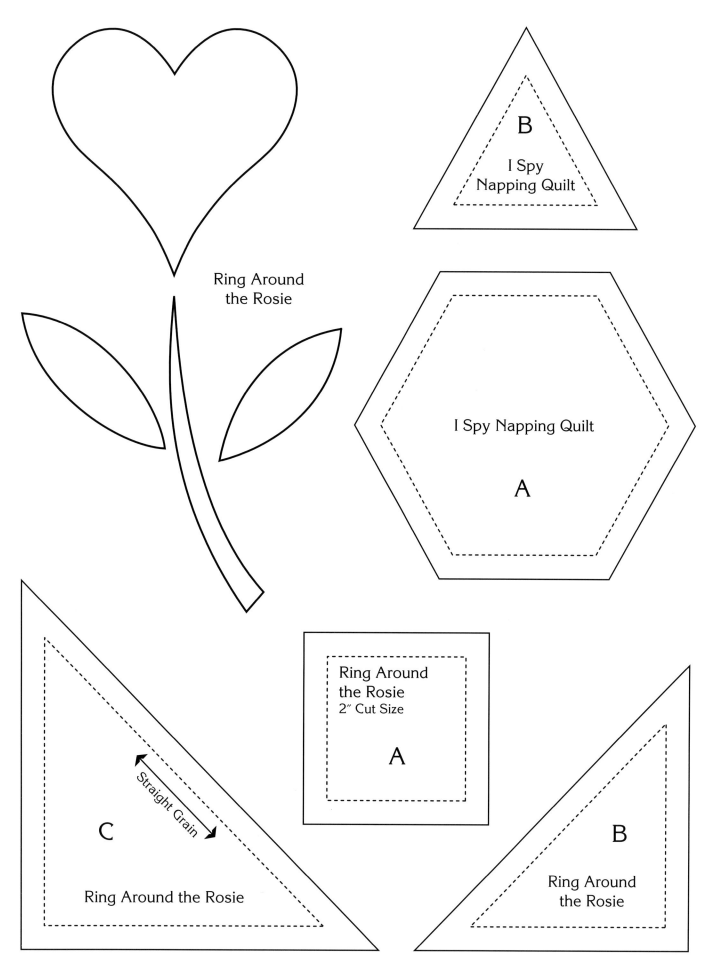

Ring Around
the Rosie

B
I Spy
Napping Quilt

I Spy Napping Quilt

A

Ring Around
the Rosie
2″ Cut Size

A

Straight Grain

C

Ring Around the Rosie

B

Ring Around
the Rosie

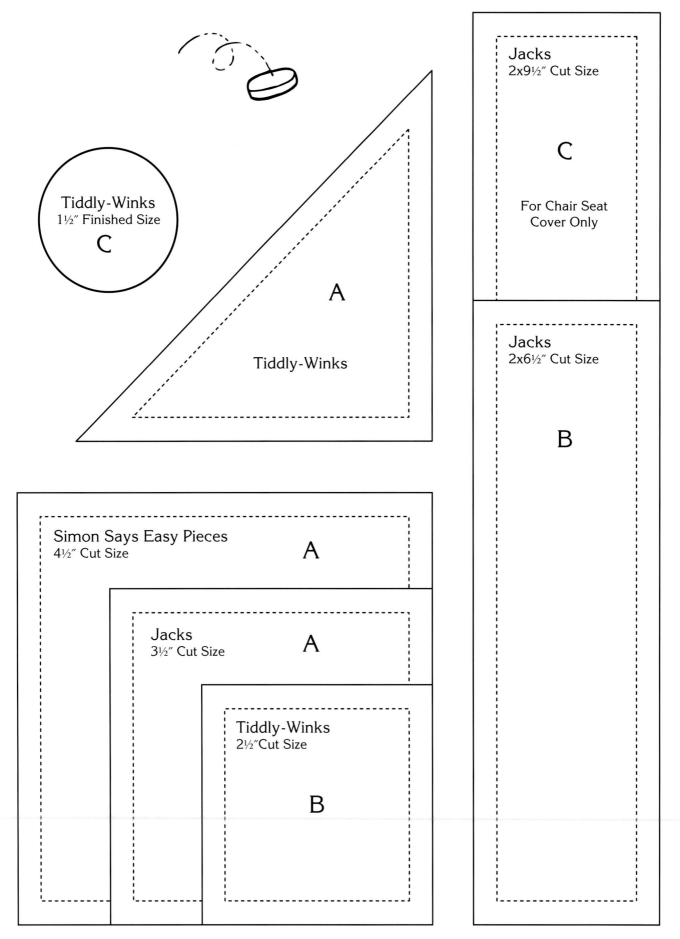

Tiddly-Winks
1½″ Finished Size
C

A

Tiddly-Winks

Jacks
2x9½″ Cut Size

C

For Chair Seat
Cover Only

Jacks
2x6½″ Cut Size

B

Simon Says Easy Pieces
4½″ Cut Size

A

Jacks
3½″ Cut Size

A

Tiddly-Winks
2½″Cut Size

B

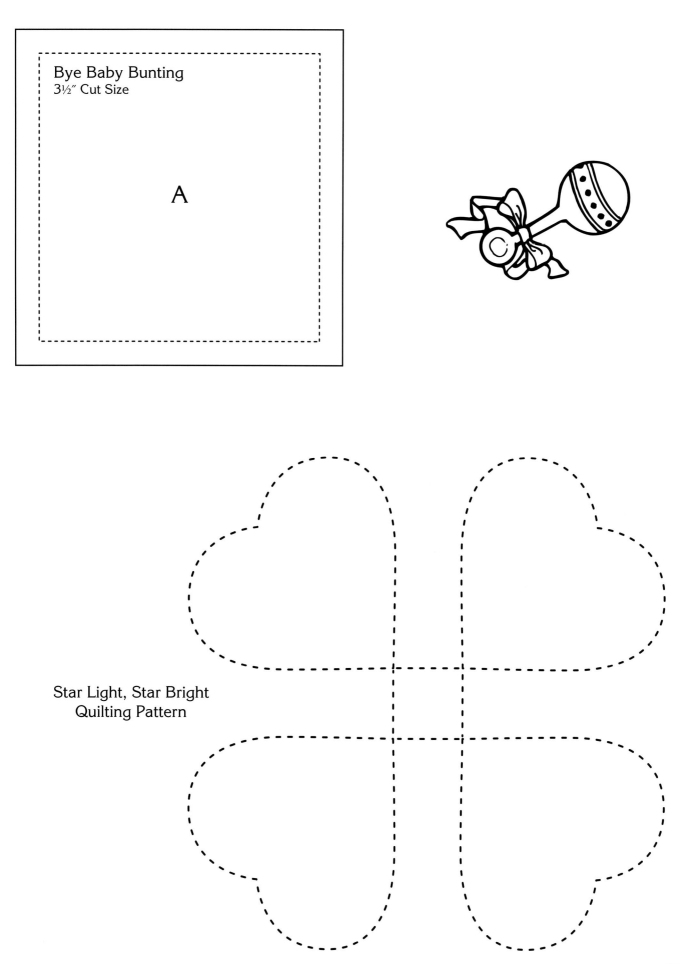

Bye Baby Bunting
3½″ Cut Size

A

Star Light, Star Bright
Quilting Pattern

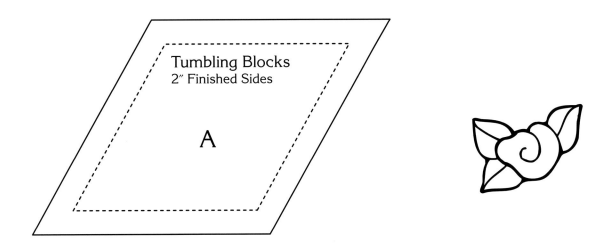

Tumbling Blocks
2″ Finished Sides

A

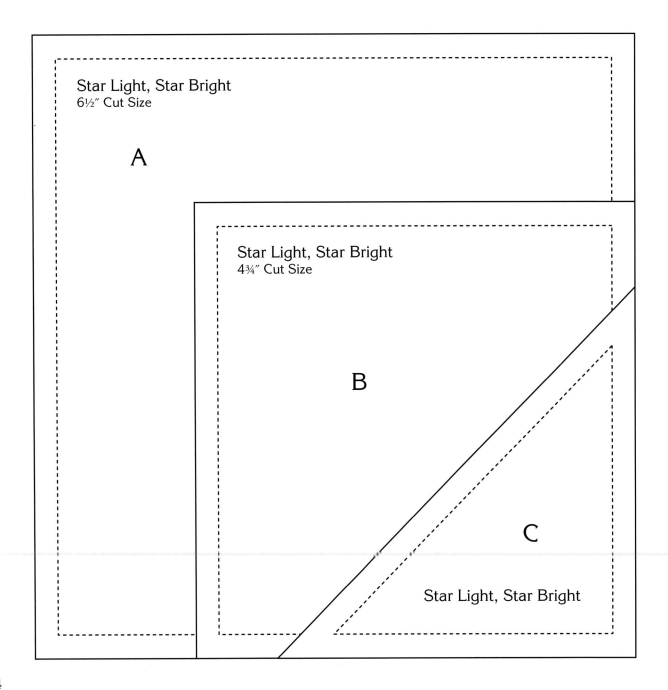

Star Light, Star Bright
6½″ Cut Size

A

Star Light, Star Bright
4¾″ Cut Size

B

C

Star Light, Star Bright

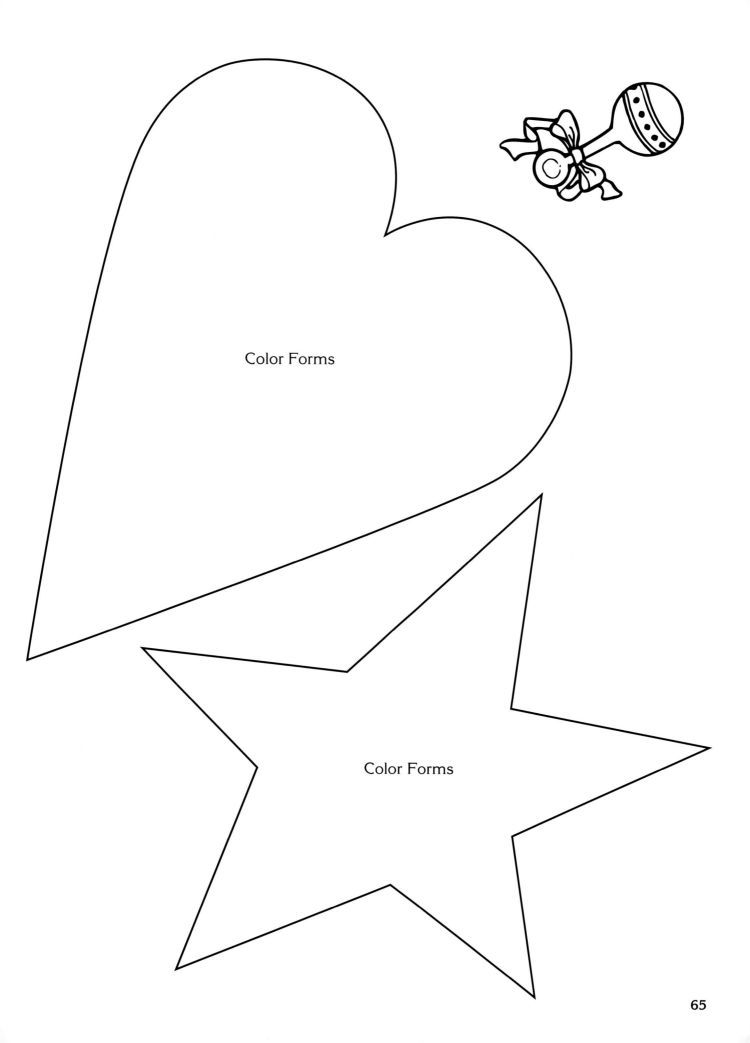

Color Forms

Color Forms

I LOVE YOU!

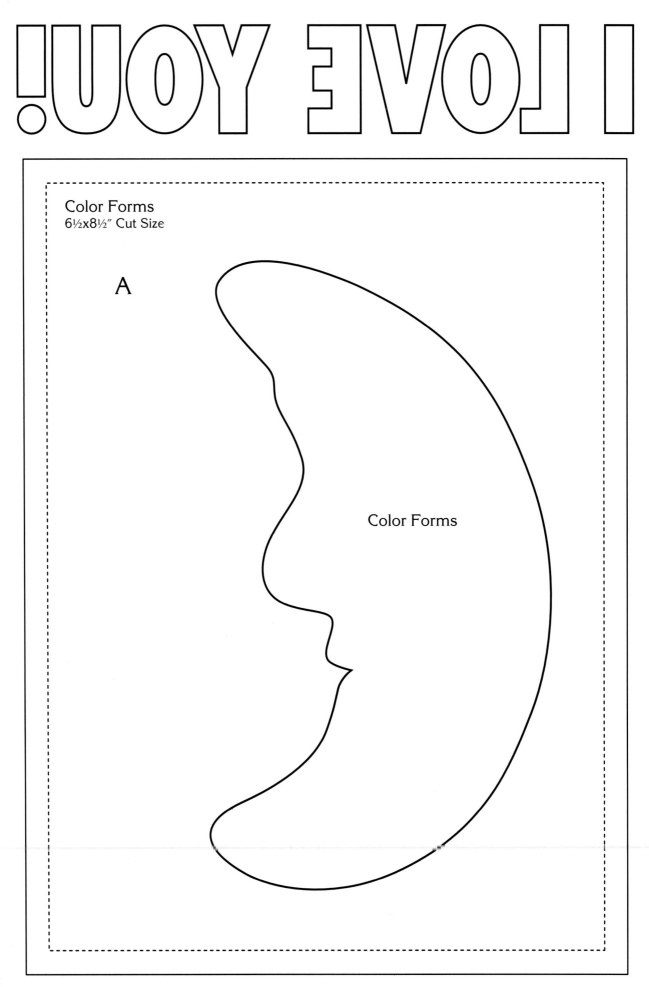

Color Forms
6½x8½″ Cut Size

A

Color Forms

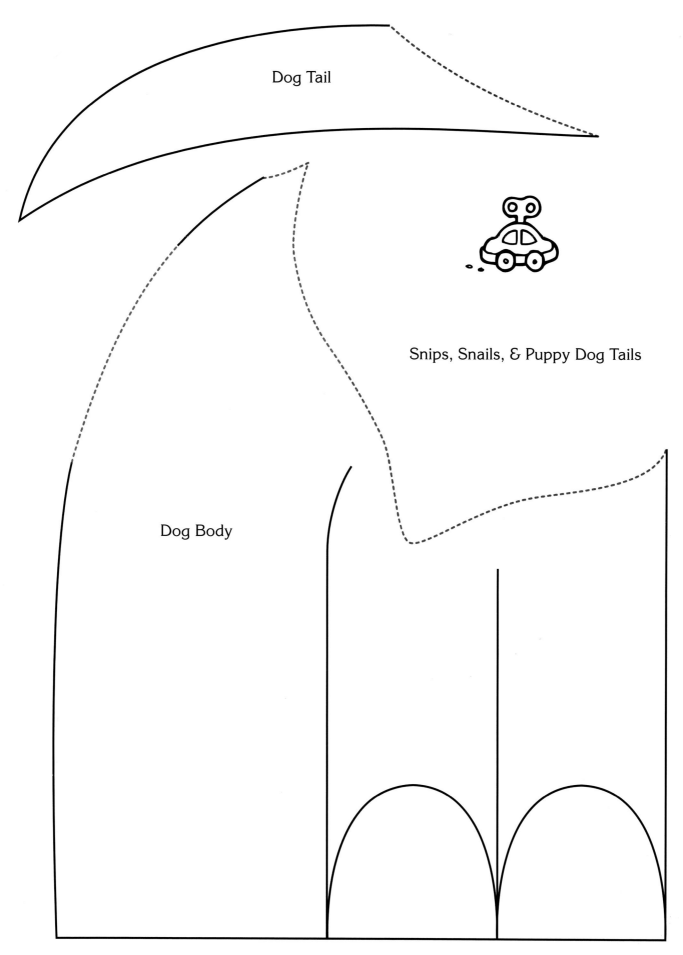

Dog Tail

Snips, Snails, & Puppy Dog Tails

Dog Body

Snips, Snails, & Puppy Dog Tails

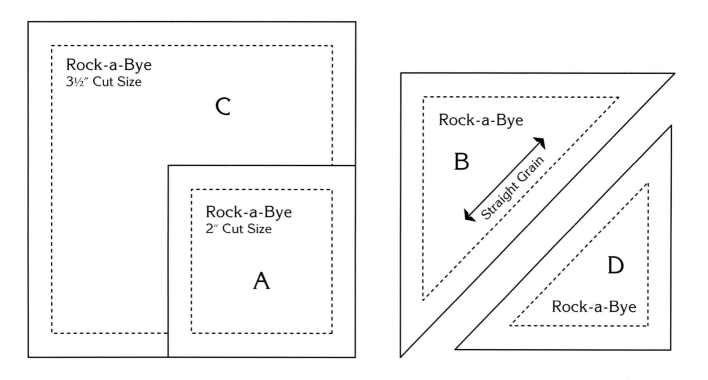

Rock-a-Bye
3½" Cut Size

C

Rock-a-Bye
2" Cut Size

A

Rock-a-Bye

B

Straight Grain

D

Rock-a-Bye

You Are My Sunshine
Quilting Pattern

PS I LOVE YOU
IT'S A GIRL
IT'S A BOY

P.S. I Love You
Girl

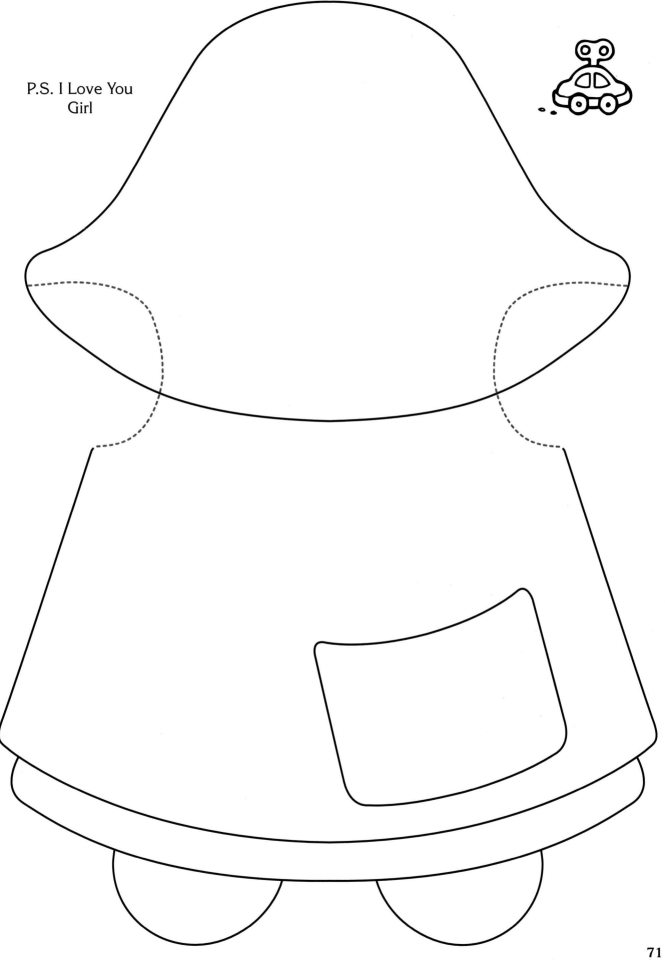

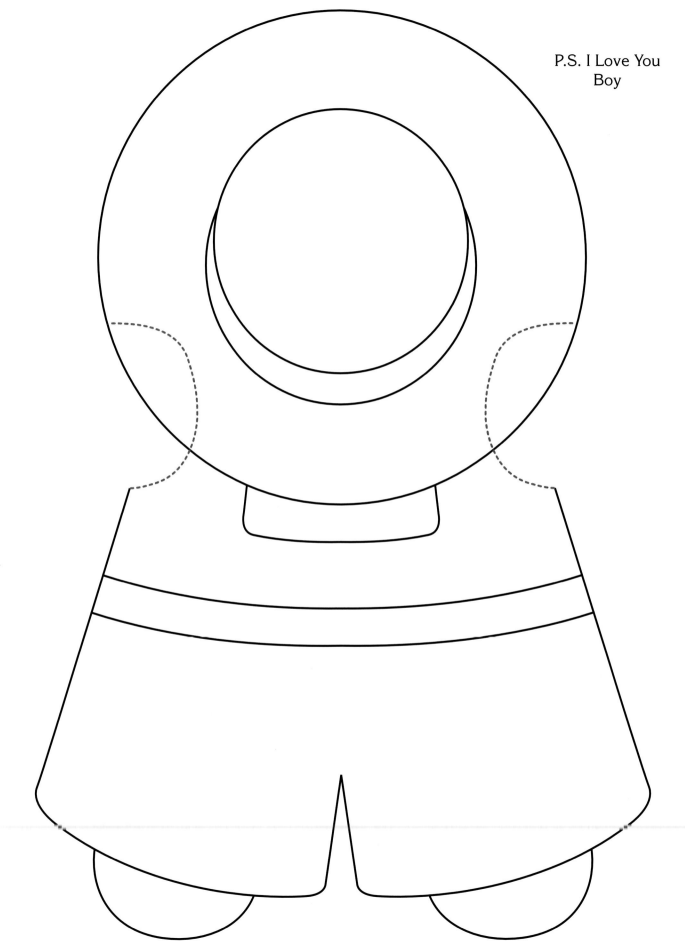

P.S. I Love You
Boy

72

Girl's Arm

Boy's Arm

P.S. I Love You

P.S. I Love You
3½" Cut Size

A

P.S.
I Love You
1½" Cut Size

B

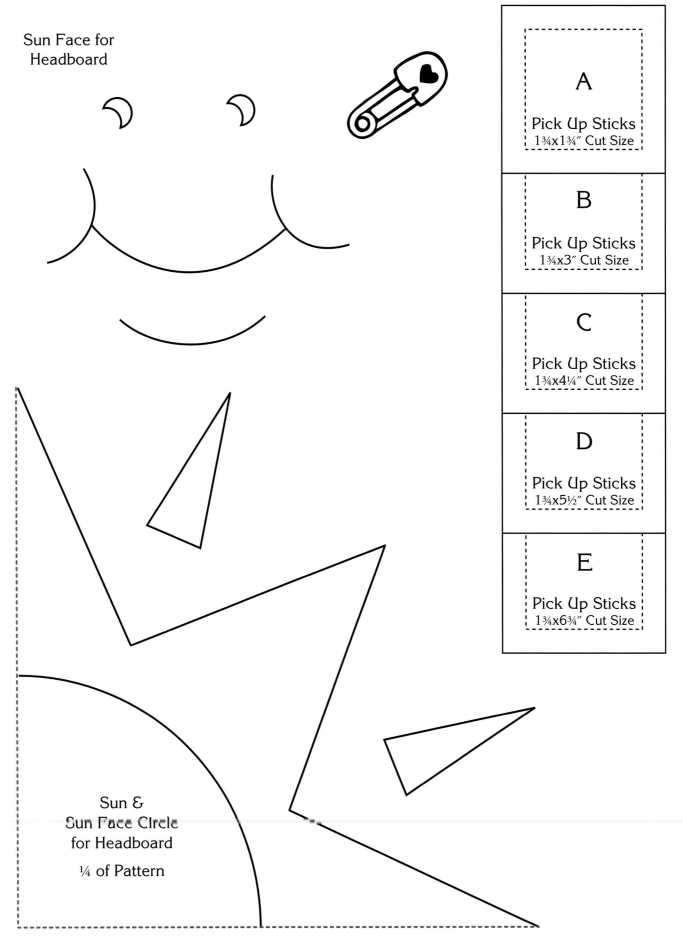

Sun Face for
Headboard

A

Pick Up Sticks
1¾x1¾" Cut Size

B

Pick Up Sticks
1¾x3" Cut Size

C

Pick Up Sticks
1¾x4¼" Cut Size

D

Pick Up Sticks
1¾x5½" Cut Size

E

Pick Up Sticks
1¾x6¾" Cut Size

Sun &
Sun Face Circle
for Headboard

¼ of Pattern

Facts of Life

Facts of Life

Cloud Pattern for
Weight & Length

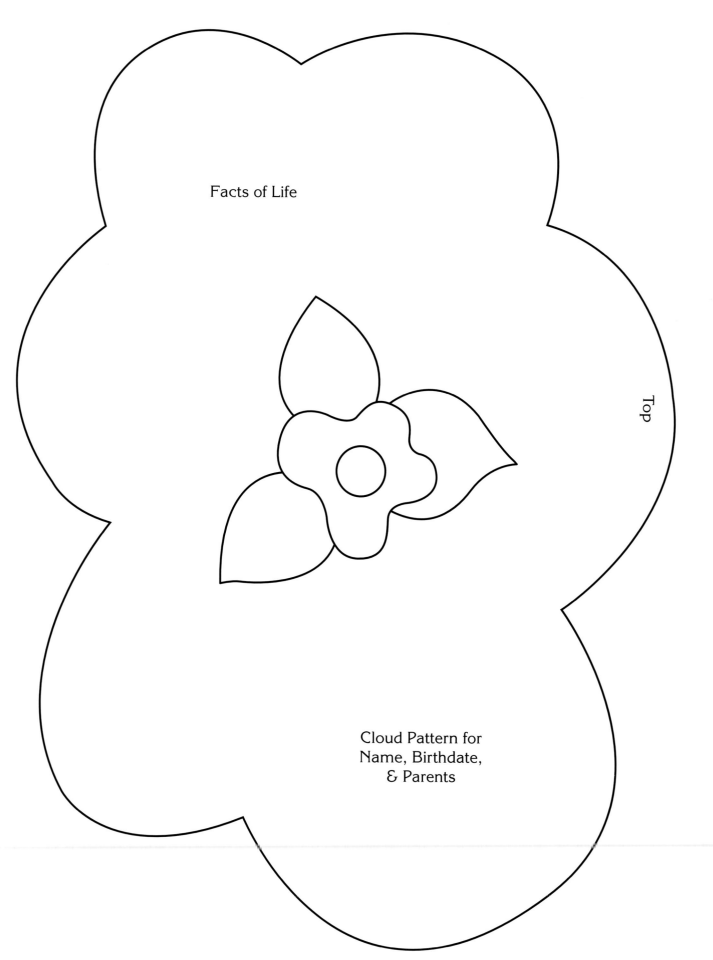

Facts of Life

Top

Cloud Pattern for
Name, Birthdate,
& Parents